Br…

• & THE BUR…

By Michael Fleet

Illustrations by
Claire S Bicknell

Please send comments, good or bad,
by email to the author at: bruinstories@gmail.com
For more information Michael Fleet • +44 7836 256693

Illustrator & Designer: Claire S Bicknell: claire@stylographics.com
Bark • Linked in • @101illustrations • +44 7940 599 455

Typeset & Designed using DyslexicLogicFont © alice.frendo@hotmail.com
Photography Jack Hudson & David Pimbblet

Dedicated with love to:

Florence, Harriet, Henry and Zoe

This book has been designed for independent readers but can be equally enjoyed by adults, parents and carers alike.

Michael Fleet

CONTENTS:

And Bruin, the family's pet German Shepherd, was lying at a right angle to Henry, with his head on the little boy's chest.

1
The Best Place In The World

It was a peaceful Sunday morning at 1 Shapleys Crescent. The Wilkie family were all there, eating from a plate of crumpets and busy doing nothing.

Mr Wilkie was on the sofa reading his paper. Mrs Wilkie was leafing through a magazine.

Florence and Harriet were on the carpet playing a game of animal Top Trumps while younger brother Henry was lying on his back, staring at the ceiling.

And Bruin, the family's pet German Shepherd, was lying at a right angle to Henry, with his head on the little boy's chest.

Mr Wilkie looked up from his paper with a satisfied expression on his face. "Where in the world would you rather be?" he asked and then straight away answered his own question.

"I wouldn't want to be anywhere else other than here, with all the family and just relaxing. Perfect!"

Henry was the first to disagree. "I'd rather be at the

park, going down the slide. Or even better, I'd like to be somewhere snowy, on a sledge." Florence then piped up. "I'd rather be playing football with my friends."

Next it was Harriet: "I'd rather be camping next to a river. Or going for a swim in the sea," she said. "But," said Mr Wilkie, "here we are, eating crumpets and just taking it easy. Is there really anywhere better than right here, right now?"

The three children all responded with a loud "Yes," and Florence went on: "There are loads of places better than right here, right now. This is just boring."

It was time for Mrs Wilkie to have her say. "What your father is trying to say is that we should be grateful for what we have here.

"We are all safe and well and happy. And best of all, the summer holidays have just started."

"I'm not happy," said Henry grumpily. "I'd rather be doing something exciting. And so would Bruin." But Bruin didn't agree.

He had been bred to be a part of the Tingleside police dog unit but from an early age he had shown himself to be much more interested in dozing and being friendly to everyone.

He thought that was much better than chasing criminals or controlling crowds by barking and snarling, like a police dog is meant to do.

He had been put up for adoption by the police

force because it was clear he would be much happier as a family pet.

That is how he came to be here, lying on the carpet and every bit one of the family.

And it meant he was the only one to agree with Mr Wilkie that lying there, relaxing, really was the best thing in the world!

Mr Wilkie went back to reading his paper. Florence and Harriet went back to their game. Mrs Wilkie went back to her magazine.

Henry went back to staring at the ceiling and Bruin carried on resting his head on Henry's chest with his eyes closed.

Suddenly Mr Wilkie started to talk again. "Here's something interesting," he said as he ruffled the paper and prepared to read aloud.

"Two children living in a village in Spain were given a metal detector and found a hoard of gold and silver coins from Roman times," he said.

"Fancy that, what a thing to happen! It says here that the coins are now going to the local museum and the children have been given a big reward," Mr Wilkie continued.

"Wow, that sounds exciting. I wonder how many coins there were and how they ever got there?" said Florence.

"I can tell you both those things," Mr Wilkie replied. "It says there were over 800 coins and it is thought they were buried by their owner for safe keeping."

"But why did the owner just leave them there?" asked Harriet.

"Perhaps he forgot where he'd buried them. Or maybe something happened to him before he could dig them up," said Mr Wilkie.

"Or maybe he was eaten by a dinosaur when he went to collect them," said Henry, sitting up and causing Bruin to also have to sit up.

"Don't be daft," said Harriet. "There weren't any dinosaurs in Roman times."

"How do you know?" demanded Henry, "Were you there?"

Mrs Wilkie put down her magazine, which Henry knew meant he was about to get a talking to.

"Now you're being silly, Henry," she started.

"We know from dinosaur experts that they died out millions of years before the Romans. So he can't have been eaten by a dinosaur."

"Well if it wasn't a dinosaur it might have been a tiger," Henry said.

"You don't get tigers in Spain either," said his mum. "You do get wolves, up in the hills," said Mr Wilkie helpfully.

"Wow," said Henry. "I bet he was eaten by wolves."

"Well," said his father. "We'll never know what happened to him or why he didn't recover the treasure later.

"All we know is that the coins were buried more than two thousand years ago and now they've been found by two children."

Mrs Wilkie put down her magazine, which Henry knew meant he was about to get a talking to.

So he tried to distract her by showing her his Cub Pet Care Badge he had recently gained showing Bruin to the pack of Cubs.

Florence gathered Harriet and Henry close
to her and Bruin stuck his nose in as well,
to make sure he wasn't missing out.

2

Florence Has A Plan!

Mr Wilkie went back to his newspaper, reading something more boring. But the story had stirred something in the Wilkie children.

Florence gathered Harriet and Henry close to her and Bruin stuck his nose in as well, to make sure he wasn't missing out.

"I wonder if we could find some buried treasure?" she whispered to them.

"We'll need a metal detector, like the children in Spain," said Harriet and the three of them suddenly all stared at their father, sitting in his armchair in his slippers and reading his Sunday newspaper.

He sensed three pairs of eyes looking at him (well, four really because Bruin was staring at him too) and he peeked around the edge of his paper to look at the children and their dog.

"Why are you staring like that? Have I got strawberry jam on the end of my nose or something?" he demanded to know. "Come along, Sam. You must know what is about to come?" Mrs Wilkie told her husband.

"I have no idea at all," he replied.

"I bet it's something to do with a metal detector," said his wife, Amy.

And sure enough, Florence was the first to blurt out: "Daaad, if we had a metal detector we might find some buried treasure."

"And when we do, we'll pay you back for the metal detector with the reward money we get," said Harriet.

"And we'll keep away from wolves," said Henry.

"But where do you think you're going to find treasure?" asked Mr Wilkie.

"It could be anywhere," said Florence.

"Yes," said Harriet. "That's why it's called treasure hunting. You have to hunt for it."

"I bet there's no treasure around here. It will be a waste of time and money," said Mr Wilkie.

But the children weren't prepared to give up the plan so easily.

"We'll never know if we don't have a go," said Florence. "There could be buried treasure right under our feet," said Henry.

"We won't know if we don't try."

Bruin agreed and he put a paw on Mr Wilkie's arm, as if trying to pull him out of his chair.

Mr Wilkie looked at Bruin and at his children and knew he had lost the argument.

And so the idea was born that the Wilkie children and Bruin should become treasure hunters, with their own metal detector!

The children were lined up at the counter, looking down at a dazzling display of coins, medals and even a shiny gold ring.

At Tom Tucker's Treasure Cabin

Two days later Mr Wilkie, the children and Bruin were at Tom Tucker's Treasure Cabin in the High Street.

The children were lined up at the counter, looking down at a dazzling display of coins, medals and even a shiny gold ring.

"Wow," said Henry. "Look at all this treasure."

Mr Tucker got down from his stool and walked over to stand behind the counter.

"All this was found within 10 miles of this shop," he told the children and Bruin.

Mr Wilkie came over to see what the children were looking at. "What, even the gold ring?" he asked Mr Tucker.

"Yes, even that. It was found by my son, Billy, using one of these metal detectors," Mr Tucker said, at the same time reaching to a shelf behind him to get down one of the metal detectors.

"He'd only been out metal detecting a couple of times when he discovered it.

"We reckon it's at least a hundred years old but just in case it belonged to someone we reported it to the police and put a notice in the window. No-one has come forward to claim it.

"And the brilliant thing is, this isn't even one of our expensive metal detectors. It's a great one to start on."

"It looks really cool daddy," said Harriet.

She looked up at Mr Tucker and asked "How much is it?"

"Well," he replied. "It's normally £59 but at the moment there's £10 off and we're also giving away a spade and a canvas bag for putting anything you find in.

"And I tell you what, I'll even add a book with the best local places to find treasure and lots of tips.

"The book alone is normally £9.99," Mr Tucker told them. He could tell the children were keen but it was up to their father to decide whether or not to buy.

The three children gathered around Mr Wilkie and promised to pay him back from any treasure they found.

Even Bruin joined in, tilting his head and whining gently to try to encourage Mr Wilkie to do the purchase of the metal detector.

"Well, what do you think? You won't find it cheaper anywhere else. Not even on the internet," Mr Tucker said.

Mr Wilkie looked down at the pleading eyes of his children and of Bruin.

"What can I do? It's a deal!" he told Mr Tucker.

"You won't regret it," said Mr Tucker, reaching for a metal detector still in its box and adding the spade, canvas bag and book.

"And all that comes to just £49," he told Mr Wilkie, who passed over a credit card to complete the purchase.

"A very wise choice," said Mr Tucker. "Who knows what you'll find? There's treasure out there, it's just waiting to be discovered," he added.

The children were clearly excited by their new metal detector and the extra things it came with and they sorted out who should carry what.

Harriet took the box with the metal detector in it, Florence picked up the spade and the book and Henry slung the dark brown canvas bag over his shoulder.

They left the shop saying a cheery goodbye to Mr Tucker. "Now we're proper treasure hunters!" said Harriet as they set off back to their car.

"I can't wait to start hunting," said Henry. "Who knows what we'll find!"

It was Henry's turn next for the detector and he found a tin can.

The First "Treasure" Hunt

Once they arrived home the excited children unpacked the metal detector and inserted the battery so it was ready for operation.

"I'll go first because I'm the oldest," said Florence, quickly.

"You two can hide some metal things and I'll see if I can find them."

Henry went to the cutlery drawer and pulled out some spoons to hide, while Harriet went to the drawer where things like pins and paper clips were kept.

"She'll never find these," she thought to herself while picking up two pins and two paper clips.

Florence closed her eyes and Henry went in to the sitting room to hide one of the spoons under a cushion, another under the rug and one wedged down the side of the sofa.

Harriet, though, crept silently out of the back door and hid the pins and paper clips in different parts of the garden.

When she crept back into the kitchen Florence still had her eyes closed. "Are you ready yet?" she asked.

And when her brother and sister said they were, she opened her eyes, switched on the metal detector and began to sweep it across the floor.

"I don't think they'll have left anything in here," Florence said to herself and moved into the sitting room.

The metal detector gently hummed while it was swept from side to side as Florence moved closer to the rug, under which Henry had hidden one of the spoons.

He looked on with a worried expression as the detector swung to and fro ever nearer to where he had hidden a spoon, "Hummmm" went the detector as it searched for metal.

Then suddenly it was right over the spoon and Henry gulped as he waited for the high pitched noise which would give away the hiding place.

But nothing.

No change in tone, "Hummmmmm" went the detector as it passed right over the spoon.

Henry breathed a sigh of relief. Maybe he'd got away with it. But now Florence was right beside the settee where the second spoon was hidden and she swept it over the piece of furniture.

"Hummmmm" it went and again Henry waited for the spoon to be discovered.

But, again, nothing. No signal to reveal the spoon's hiding place.

Henry couldn't understand it and began worrying that maybe the metal detector wasn't working.

"There must be something in here somewhere," said Florence as she moved across the sitting room and closer to the cushion under which Henry had hidden the third spoon.

Surely this one would be discovered, he thought as "hummmmm" the machine inched closer and was swept left and right, getting nearer to the cushion.

Then it was right over the cushion and bound to send out a signal that it had found the spoon.

But again, nothing to indicate the spoon's hiding place and Florence moved past the cushion and towards the door.

Then, as she went past, her foot caught the edge of the cushion and sent it flying across the floor.

And there, for all the world to see, was a spoon. Florence stopped, looked at the spoon and then looked at Henry.

"Did you hide that there?" she asked her brother and he nodded his head, pleased that he had outfoxed his sister and the new metal detector.

"You numbskull," she suddenly scolded Henry.

"I'm not the numbskull," Henry replied. "You are. You didn't find the spoons."

"Of course I didn't," she told him. "These spoons aren't made of metal. They're the plastic ones we take on picnics."

"Oh," said Henry. "Won't it find plastic ones?"

"Of course it won't. It's called a metal detector because it finds metal. Doh!"

At this point Mrs Wilkie entered the room to find the children still bickering. "Right," she said.

"Henry, go and find three proper metal spoons and then put them where the plastic ones were and we'll see if the metal detector is working."

So Henry did as he was told and seconds later the metal detector was giving a satisfying "beeeep" each time it located one of the metal spoons. "That's more like it," said Florence.

"It works!" shouted Henry, delighted to see that the metal detector wasn't faulty after all.

"Now you have to find my things," said Harriet, with a smug look on her face, convinced they were too well hidden. "I'll give you a clue. They're not inside the house."

"Right," said Florence as she headed into the garden and started sweeping the metal detector across the grass and the flower beds.

Within 20 seconds the detector turned from "hummmmm" to "beeeep" and Florence got to her knees and started to scrape away earth in a flower bed.

"I've got something," she shouted as she dug out an old, rusty nail. "It's not treasure, but it is metal!" she said as the nail went in to her bag and she started sweeping the ground again.

Twenty minutes later she had found the pins and paper clips as well as some bottle tops, an old spring and, the star of the show, a 50p coin.

"Wow," said Henry as the coin was dug up. "That's real treasure!"

"It sure is," said Florence. "And now we know the metal detector works we can go on a proper treasure hunt. I wonder what we'll find."

But her excitement was soon ended as Mr Wilkie held out his hand. "I'll take that 50 pence," he said. "Now you only have to find another £48.50 and the metal detector is paid for with treasure!"

Florence handed over the coin but even doing that couldn't dampen the children's enthusiasm for their new treasure hunting metal detector adventure. "My go next," said Harriet and she closed her eyes tight shut as Florence and Henry set off to hide some things.

Henry made sure he used metal this time and his collection of three badges were quickly uncovered once Harriet set off on the hunt.

Florence, though, was super crafty. Two drawing pins were hidden in the kitchen and quickly found by Harriet.

For her third piece of "treasure" Florence chose a paper clip. "This will cause Harriet problems," she chuckled to herself as she sneakily attached the paper clip to Bruin's collar.

So, as Bruin followed Harriet while she used the metal detector to find the third piece of treasure, little did she know it was always behind her!

After half an hour of hunting, right through the house and in the garden, Harriet sat on one of the garden chairs.

"I don't think you've hidden a third thing," she told Florence. "Well, I have!" Florence insisted with a smug look on her face.

"You thought you were being clever hiding your things in the garden. This one's even cleverer," she told her sister.

Harriet was getting grumpy at not finding the third thing while her sister looked so pleased with herself.

She decided a cuddle with Bruin was what she needed and Bruin was happy to come over as soon as he was called.

Harriet wrapped her arms around Bruin's neck. "At least you're not being mean," she told him as Bruin snuggled in.

Harriet wrapped her arms around Bruin's neck. "At least you're not being mean," she told him as Bruin snuggled in.

And then she saw it – a blue paperclip attached to Bruin's blue collar! "That sneaky sister of mine!" Harriet said to herself.

Florence had gone inside with Henry so didn't see Harriet spring to her feet and switch the metal detector back on.

She gently put it next to Bruin's collar and "beeeep" it went off.

Harriet pulled the paperclip off and marched into the sitting room where Florence was quietly sitting reading a book.

"Hard cheese clever clogs!" Harriet announced as she stood in front of Florence with her arms crossed and one fist clenched. Slowly she opened her fist and there was the paper clip.

Florence was astonished to see it. "You found it. I don't believe it!" she said.

"Where was it?" asked Henry and Harriet told him. "That's mean," said Henry. "You'd better not do that when I have to search."

The girls both promised they wouldn't and when it was Henry's turn they made sure their things were simpler to find.

He was still excited every time he found something though and all three children couldn't wait for their first proper treasure hunt!

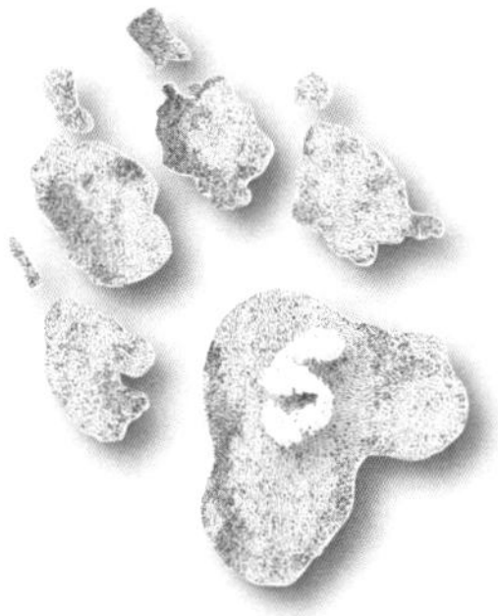

Off To The Beach

The next day was Wednesday and the children were wide awake by 7.30am to start planning their treasure hunt.

They all crowded into Florence's bed and Henry was sent downstairs to fetch the book with tips on finding local treasure.

He reappeared a minute later with the book and with Bruin who didn't want to miss out if there was going to be some excitement and he jumped up on to the bed as well.

The first tip in the book was to try the beach and they decided that was where they would go for their first treasure hunt.

"You can come too," Harriet told Bruin. "We might need you to be our guard dog to protect the treasure."

"And you can help with the digging," said Henry.

"It's going to be great. I wonder what we'll find. Come on, let's get dressed," said Florence.

Ten minutes later the children were washed and dressed and downstairs for breakfast.

Harriet packed a picnic bag with bottles of water and flapjacks she and mum had made a couple of days earlier (plus dog biscuits for Bruin) and straight after breakfast the three adventurers and Bruin set off for the beach, Florence having gone upstairs to tell their parents where they were going.

"Just don't be disappointed if you don't find anything valuable," warned dad.

But that was quickly forgotten and the excitement grew as the 10 minute walk to the beach was nearing an end.

By the time they were on the sand they were convinced they would find some coins at least. "There must be loads of treasure around here," said Henry.

Walking in a line with Harriet in the middle with the detector they swept it across the sand till "beeeeep" it sounded the alert that something was under the sand.

The three children all dropped to their knees and Henry passed the spade to Florence so she could scrape and dig to start searching.

"I told you there'd be loads of treasure," said an excited Henry.

But a few seconds later they found what was sounding the alert: A metal bottle top! "Well at least it worked," said Florence.

"Come on, let's keep looking."

It was Henry's turn next for the detector and he found a tin can.

Then it was Florence, who found a broken hair slide with a metal clip.

"It's not exactly treasure," Harriet complained loudly and after another hour of searching they'd discovered two more bottle tops, two more cans, a metal buckle from a belt and a penny coin. The three of them sat down for their flapjacks and water.

A plastic bowl was produced and filled with water for Bruin and he happily tucked into the three dog biscuits.

Maybe this treasure hunting wasn't going to be as easy as we hoped, thought Florence.

But she didn't say anything to the others and they cheered themselves up with the thought that it was only their first try.

After their snack they found more tin cans and a jam jar lid and as they trudged off the beach they put their "treasure" in to the bin.

The only thing that could be called anywhere near proper treasure was the penny coin and that was put into the special bag. Despite the disappointment they began to look forward to their next expedition.

They tried again on Wednesday afternoon (three more drinks cans, a bit of tin foil and a fishing hook) and again on Saturday (another two cans, a broken tin opener and a small toy car without any wheels).

By now the children were starting to think they'd never find anything that was interesting or valuable.

"There must be something good here. Maybe we'll find it tomorrow," said Henry and Bruin gave him an encouraging lick.

Florence and Harriet though were less enthusiastic about another day's treasure hunting instead of going out with their friends.

That evening the girls decided they would be better off doing something else with their Sunday rather than returning to the beach for more treasure hunting.

But Henry did his best to keep up the excitement of what they might find. "Just remember those children in Spain!" he said.

By now they had searched a large part of the beach and were about to start exploring the far corner, near some rock pools.

"If I was going to bury something on the beach, that's where I would do it.

"Imagine if some Roman treasure is there and we just left it for someone else to find," said Henry excitedly,

Bruin gave a gentle, encouraging whine as if to say "I'm with you Henry!"

Mr Wilkie tried to keep the excitement going by saying "some people wait years before they find something interesting or valuable" but that certainly didn't help!

"We don't want to spend years looking before we find something interesting," said Florence, and Harriet agreed.

Henry though wouldn't listen to their grumbles and after five more minutes of pestering, the girls agreed to give it one more go the next day.

"But if we don't find anything I'm not spending the rest of the summer holidays looking," said Harriet grumpily.

Mr Wilkie realised he had not helped with his warning that it could take years before something was found and as Henry and Bruin looked at him and shook their heads, he thought it best to keep quiet!

There was still some time before tea so Florence and Harriet decided they should make the most of the rest of the day. They went off to the park, leaving Henry and Bruin behind this time.

When they reached the park, Florence put down her football and kicked it as hard as she could.

It went flying over Harriet's head and she had to turn and run to fetch it. She wanted to kick it straight back to Florence but it was not a good shot and the ball went up in the air and then went spinning towards the woods at the edge of the park.

"I'll get it," shouted Florence and she ran to where the ball was last seen as it headed towards the trees.

For years the children of Tingleside had been wary of the woods and there were stories of a strange old man who lived there in a cave.

He was said to have long dirty fingernails, straggly hair and warts on his nose and he was said to have frightened any children who dared enter the woods.

There was even a story that he had put one child in a pot of boiling water!

The parents of the town remembered the story from their own childhood and tried to reassure today's children that it was only made up.

But as she stood at the edge of the woods, Florence remembered the story. She peered into the woods, looking for the ball but couldn't see it anywhere.

"How far did it go?" she shouted to Harriet.
"I don't know,"

Harriet replied. "The wind carried it into the middle of the woods."

There was only one thing for it – Florence had to enter the woods and look for the ball.

"It's only a story, it's only a story," she told herself over and over as she thought of the strange old man.

She bravely took a step into the woods and straight away the thick leaves blocked out most of the sun.

Where the light did get through it made dark shadows across the path which went deeper into the woods.

It looked to Florence as if the shadows took on a life of their own and they moved to and fro.

One step at a time, Florence walked on looking for the ball.

The further in she went, the darker it became and the noise of the town, with its traffic and people's voices, disappeared, replaced with an eerie silence.

Florence looked all about her but there was no sign of the ball.

She stepped on a fallen branch and it made a loud cracking sound and suddenly a resting rabbit shot out in front of her, making her jump.

Her imagination made her hear all sorts of noises, some of them sounding like footsteps.

Was someone following her? "Hello," she called out. "Is anyone there?"

There was no answer, just the sound of the wind whistling through the trees.

"Harriet...is that you?" she called out, hoping that the noises were coming from her sister. But there was no reply.

On she went, into the heart of the wood and the path disappeared under thick grass and weeds.

She felt a chill down her neck as the woods became darker and darker and the noise of the wind started to sound like voices.

She was sure she heard her name being called "Florence, Florence," it went but she ordered her mind to stop playing tricks.

"It's only a story, it's only a story," she repeated.

But hard as she might try, she couldn't stop thinking about the old man of the woods who frightened children. Was he watching her?

Suddenly she spotted her black and white football, sitting in the middle of a bush.

She went towards it and as she reached out for the football...she lost her balance.

Outside the woods Harriet was starting to get really concerned.

Her sister had been gone for more than 20 minutes and every time she called out her name there was no response.

She knew the stories of the strange old man and

started to get worried.

There was only one thing for it..Bruin!

Giving one last shout for Florence's name and calling out that she'd be back soon she ran home as fast as she could.

She burst through the kitchen door shouting, "quick, bring Bruin."

Henry and Bruin heard the commotion and quick as a flash joined Harriet in the kitchen. "What's the matter?" asked Henry.

Harriet quickly explained that Florence had vanished into the woods. "We need Bruin to find her," she told Henry.

Straight away the pair of them and Bruin set off for the park.

As soon as they reached the woods, Harriet showed Bruin where Florence had entered the path looking for the football.

Bruin stepped forward and tilted his head from side to side as he looked into the woods.

"Go and find Florence!" Harriet told Bruin.

Bruin immediately ran into the woods and quickly picked up Florence's scent.

Deeper and deeper he went, his nose hovering just above the ground as he followed the trail.

Suddenly Florence spotted Bruin.

"Bruin, Bruin, over here," she shouted and Bruin ran to her and gave her a reassuring lick.

"I can't find the way out," she told him.

She had hold of the football but her arms were scratched from the thick twigs which had wrapped themselves around the football.

She had fallen into the bush as she reached out for the ball and again her mind had played tricks. Did someone push her?

Thankfully, she had managed to stop thinking that but as she had stood by the bush with the football she had become frightened that she was hopelessly lost.

The path was covered in weeds and was impossible to follow, meaning she had no idea about how to get out of the woods.

But now Bruin was here to help her and having no path was not a problem for him!

He put his nose close to the ground and simply followed the route back out of the woods, with Florence hanging on to his collar.

On and on they went until the darkness began to be replaced by daylight and it was clear they were at the edge of the woods.

And then, suddenly, they were out of the woods and back in the sunshine. And there, waiting for them, were Harriet and Henry.

The pair of them rushed forward to Florence

and wrapped their arms around her.

"Thank goodness you're alright," said Harriet. "But look at your arms. They're full of cuts and scratches."

"That happened when I got the ball out from a bush. I fell in to the middle of it.

"I must admit I was getting worried after that but then I saw Bruin. He saved me!" said Florence with a smile.

It was an eventful end to the day and by the time the children and Bruin returned home it was time for tea.

Suddenly another day's "boring" treasure hunting looked like a good idea to Florence. Anything to stop having to go into the woods again, she thought to herself!

6

Something is found

Only Henry and Bruin were up at 7.30 the next morning.

Florence and Harriet stayed firmly in bed as the sun began to creep higher in the sky and it was nearly 11 before they were up and dressed and finishing breakfast.

"Come on slowcoaches," Henry told them as he waited by the back door with metal detector, spade and bag ready for action and with Bruin sitting patiently beside him.

"Alright, alright, we're coming," said Harriet as she again prepared their picnic bag with water, flapjacks and dog biscuits.

The two sisters made sure Henry knew he was lucky to get them on another treasure hunt but they were loyal to their brother and to Bruin and soon after 11.30 the little party set off for the beach again.

When they arrived they headed for the far corner and Florence took the first go with the detector. Within 30 seconds there was a loud "beeeeep" and guess what? Another tin can!

"Here we go again," she complained as the detector was handed to Harriet and a fresh piece of sand was swept over.

After another half an hour there was not a single alert from the detector, not even another bottle top or tin can, and Harriet announced she was going to try right beneath the cliff at the back of the beach.

"If I was going to bury something here, that's where I would choose," she announced.

Forwards and backwards went the detector but nothing was found apart from two more tin cans.

Then suddenly there was the most powerful "beeeep" they had ever heard and the children and Bruin surrounded the area where the sound came from.

"It's probably a load of tin cans tied together," said Florence grumpily as she used the spade to dig, but she couldn't see anything.

"Put the detector down here again," she told Harriet and as soon as it was put into the hole it sounded another really loud "beeeeep."

This time Bruin took over and used his front paws to dig frantically in the hole, spraying sand behind him.

Henry was the first to spot something. "What's that?" he called out as something black and flat started to be uncovered. "Go on Bruin, keep going," Henry said and within seconds more black metal was uncovered to reveal a small square box with a handle on the top.

"Well done Bruin, now stand back," said Harriet as she lay on her tummy so she could reach down into the hole and lift out the box.

"Wow," said Henry, "That looks like it could be real treasure."

The children were all on their knees and put the box in the middle of their circle.

"You stand guard, Bruin," Henry said and Bruin walked around the little group, making sure no-one else could get near.

"What do you think's inside it?" asked Henry.

"I don't know. It's locked. But it looks pretty old," said Florence.

Harriet picked up the box and shook it.

"There's definitely something inside. I can hear it," she said to growing excitement from the three children.

"There's no key anywhere so I don't know how we'll get inside it."

Florence told her: "We'll take it home and get daddy to open it.

"Now, this is important, when we walk back don't let on that we've found something," she told the others. "Just remain calm and normal."

She put the box inside the canvas bag and the three of them walked back casually, as if saying "nothing interesting here," and Bruin trotted behind, looking from side to side for any noseyparkers who might be around.

Once they were off the beach, the children and Bruin couldn't resist breaking in to a run to get home as quickly as possible.

Once they reached the house they piled in through the kitchen door all shouting: "Dad, dad, get here quickly."

Mr and Mrs Wilkie both came into the kitchen as quickly as they could.

"What's the matter? Is someone hurt?" asked Mrs Wilkie but the children were quick to reassure her.

"We're all fine," said Florence. "But we need daddy's help."

Mr Wilkie sat at the kitchen table and asked how he could help.

Harriet proudly produced the metal box from the bag and put it on the table.

"We've found some real treasure," she told him

in a triumphant voice.

Mr Wilkie examined the box, turning it from side to side and upside down.

As he did so, a loud rattle sounded from inside the box and the three children and Bruin all peered closer still, their eyes as wide as they could go.

"What's inside?" Mrs Wilkie asked.

"We don't know yet, Amy. It's locked," said Mr Wilkie and he reached into a cupboard to get out a tool box.

He used a big screwdriver to try to prise the lid open but it wouldn't budge.

Then he got a hammer and hit the handle of the screwdriver, forcing it deeper into the edge of the lid.

Suddenly there was a loud "pop" and the lid came open.

7

The Box of Surprises

The children, Bruin and Mr and Mrs Wilkie all peered closer, trying to see inside till Mr Wilkie told everyone to make some space.

"As the children found it, they should be the ones to discover what's inside," he announced and the box was passed down the table to be in front of Florence, Harriet, Henry and Bruin.

"I'll go first," said Florence and she put her hand inside the box.

Everything was wrapped in newspaper to keep it safe and Florence picked out the first little parcel.

The newspaper was dated June 18th 1973, showing that the box was over 50 years old and as Florence unwrapped the first package out rolled a pair of solid gold cufflinks.

"Wow," said all the children together as the shiny objects landed on the kitchen table.

Harriet went next and she pulled apart a wrapped up parcel to reveal a photograph in a silver frame with a man, a woman and a baby in the picture with the message "the three of us outside our new house" written on the back.

Henry dipped his hand in next and came up with a package which contained three big silver coins.

"This is real treasure," he said as he laid the sparkling coins on the table. "I wonder if it was put there by pirates!"

There were three more parcels and Florence opened the first one to reveal a gold fountain pen still inside its box.

On the box was written the message "Presented to Arthur Chisholm for 25 years of loyal service to Smalling & Co." She looked at Henry. "I don't think that's anything to do with pirates!" she told him.

Florence laid the pen next to the other things and Harriet opened the next parcel, which contained a beautiful pearl necklace.

Again there was a note with it, which just said "mum's pearls" and they were obviously a treasured family possession.

"This is amazing," said Harriet. The last parcel was smaller than the others and Henry picked it up and unwrapped the newspaper.

This piece of newspaper was torn from the front page and contained the name "Chis" and what looked like part of an address, "3 Boyle." Henry laid the piece of newspaper to one side and unwrapped some brightly coloured tissue paper to reveal the greatest piece of treasure.

It was a diamond and sapphire engagement ring and it sparkled in the sunlight coming through the kitchen window.

Henry gulped as he saw the shining jewel and he gently laid it alongside the other pieces from the box. "Look at all this treasure," he said.

"It's awesome," said Harriet. "I wonder how it got there?" "I don't know," said Florence. "But our next job is to see if we can find out who it belonged to and get it back to them."

Mrs Wilkie looked on and smiled. "That's a great thing to say Florence. Just imagine how wonderful it would be if you could get all this back to whoever owns it."

Henry didn't agree. "I think we should keep it. Finders keepers." Harriet shook her head gently. "We can't do that Henry. This must be really important to whoever owns it. We must find them and give it back." Henry shrugged his shoulders. "OK. I suppose you're right," he said.

And so the children knew that the next part of their treasure hunting adventure would be getting it back to its owner. But how easy was that going to be?

Little did they know what excitement lay ahead for the three of them!

The Next Part of The Adventure Begins

The children, Mr and Mrs Wilkie and Bruin sat around the kitchen table looking at the pieces of treasure laid out in front of the family

There was the pearl necklace, the photograph in a silver frame, three silver coins, a gold fountain pen, a pair of gold cufflinks and the diamond and sapphire engagement ring.

They all sat in stunned silence looking at what they had found until Florence was the first one to speak.

"There are two real clues here," she said, rubbing her chin.

"The pen is marked to Arthur Chisholm from Smalling and Co. He must have worked for them. Do we know anything about that company?"

Florence then picked up the torn piece of newspaper with "Chis 3 Boyle" written on it.

"This is the other clue. Chis must be for Mr Chisholm. And isn't there a Boyle Terrace somewhere in town?

"It must mean that what we have to do is go there and find number 3," she said.

Mrs Wilkie then spoke. "I'll be amazed if they still live there. But it's a start," she said.

"I've never heard of Smalling and Co but I know someone who might know about them.

"Mr Hardacre two doors down from us has lived here all his life. You could ask him," she said.

The children wasted no time and as soon as they had Bruin on his lead they headed to Mr Hardacre's house and were knocking on his door.

A minute later the elderly gentleman opened the door and looked down at his group of callers.

He was in his carpet slippers and wearing a dark grey cardigan, with a brightly coloured cravat (a sort of silk scarf) at his neck.

"Well, well, well," he said. "To what do we owe the pleasure of seeing you youngsters. And Bruin as well! It must be something important."

"It is important," said Harriet. "We're hoping you can help us."

Henry then piped up "because you're so old,"

A minute later
the elderly
gentleman opened
the door and
looked down at
his group
of callers.

he said and was given a shake by Florence to stop him saying anything else rude.

"We just need some information from someone who…." she thought hard about how to put it more politely.

"Er, who has lived here a long time," Florence told Mr Hardacre.

She was really saying the same thing but in a more polite way.

"Well, I have lived here a long time so, if I can, of course I'll help you," said Mr Hardacre.

Then looking at Henry, he added with a chuckle "sometimes it's useful to be as old as me," and he gave the six-year-old a friendly wink before inviting the children and Bruin inside.

The three children sat in a line on the settee with Bruin on the floor beside them and Mr Hardacre sat in his favourite chair, one which had a lever he could pull to bring up a support for his legs.

There were photographs around the room, some of Mr Hardacre and his wife, who had died two years ago.

Others were of his grown up children and his grandchildren and behind Mr Hardacre was a bookcase full of books.

He noticed Florence looking at the books and he told her:

"I've collected hundreds of books over the

years," he said. "Of course you can get all the information inside them within a few seconds on the internet these days."

Henry again chimed in: "Wow, I didn't think old people knew how to use the internet."

"Oh, you'd be surprised at what we can do. I've even got one of those smart phone thingies," Mr Hardacre told him with a chuckle and Henry was very impressed.

"Now, what can I do to help you three young-uns?" he asked.

Florence stood up and stepped towards Mr Hardacre's chair.

"We're trying to find someone who used to work at a place called Smalling and Co. Have you heard of it?" she asked him.

Mr Hardacre thought for a few moments and then said, "Yes, I remember Smallings. They used to make things out of steel.

"Metal rods and ballbearings, that type of thing. But goodness me, that's going back a few years. They must have closed down nearly 40 years ago." "Did you know someone called Arthur Chisholm, who worked there?" asked Florence.

Again Mr Hardacre had a think, muttering the name "Arthur Chisholm" several times and again after a few moments his face lit up and he spoke, "Well I never, I do remember an Arthur Chisholm," he said.

"I played cricket with him for Tingleside many years ago. I don't know what could have happened to him though."

Mr Hardacre then went silent and was thinking again, tapping his fingers on his chin.

Suddenly he clapped his hands together and beamed as if a new thought had hit him like a bolt from the blue.

"Hang on a mo. I know someone who used to work at Smallings. I wonder if he knew him," he suddenly said.

He got up out of his chair and went to a drawer in his sideboard and took out an address book.

"I should have his number here," he said.

He started humming to himself as he looked through the book before suddenly saying: "There he is, Harry Rowntree. Let's give him a ring!"

He picked up his phone and reading the number in the book, dialled it.

A few seconds later he said into the phone: "Hello Harry, it's Jack. How are you?"

The children couldn't hear Harry's reply but heard Mr Hardacre then say "Harry, in your time at Smallings did you know a chap called Arthur Chisholm? He worked there for quite a few years apparently."

There was silence in the room as Harry spoke

and then Mr Hardacre said. "That's great. Do you know where he lived?"

Again, there was silence in the room broken only by Mr Hardacre saying things like "Right," and "I see," in response to what Harry was saying until he said goodbye and turned to face the children.

"Well, Harry did know him but said he died years ago. He was married to a lady called Rita and they had a son, called Matthew," he told them.

"Did he know where they lived?" asked Harriet.

"They lived in Boyle Terrace but Harry thinks they moved from there and he doesn't know where to. That's as much as he knows," said Mr Hardacre.

"That must be the 3 Boyle on the newspaper. We'll have to go there next," said Florence before getting to her feet.

She walked over to Mr Hardacre and told him: "Thank you so much for all your help. You've been very kind and helpful. And please pass on our thanks to Harry."

"Oh, I'm just glad we were able to get you some information. Good luck with it!" Mr Hardacre told her with a smile.

The children left, chattering excitedly about the progress they were making. The investigation into the treasure box had begun!

9

What Next?

The children and Bruin returned home to discuss what they had discovered.

Florence took the lead, standing in front of the other two ready to present the evidence they had so far uncovered.

Harriet and Henry sat at the kitchen table as Florence slowly paced to and fro in front of them and Bruin.

She imagined she was a detective like Sherlock Holmes, going over the evidence so far.

"What we know is that the box belonged to a man called Arthur Chisholm and his wife, Rita.

"They had a son called Matthew and at the time they were living at 3 Boyle Terrace.

"Mr Chisholm worked for Smalling and Co. which closed down about 40 years ago and we know that he died some time after that," she said.

Harriet then said: "I think our next job is to go to 3 Boyle Terrace and see what we can discover. We'll take Bruin who can make sure we are all right."

Mrs Wilkie was getting out the ingredients for one of the cakes she made in her business but was starting to get concerned.

She said she would drive the children to Boyle Terrace and she and Bruin would wait in the car while they went to investigate.

The children protested that they didn't need anyone to go with them but Mrs Wilkie said: "You never know who lives there now.

"I'm sure everything will be fine but I'll feel much happier if I can go with you, just to make sure you're safe".

"I'll keep out of the way and it will still be your investigation," she told them.

Bruin went and stood beside Mrs Wilkie, which was his way of saying "I think that's a good plan," and the children all agreed.

They had to have lunch first and sat down to sandwiches and orange squash.

Straight afterwards they all piled in to Mrs Wilkie's car to find 3 Boyle Terrace, which was near the town centre.

They drove slowly down the street, counting down the numbers on the doors until Florence cried out "there it is," and they pulled up outside number 3.

It was an old fashioned terraced house but it looked like it had new windows and a new roof and had brightly coloured curtains.

"What do we do now?" asked Harriet and her mother replied:

"well, all you can do is knock on the door and see who lives there.

"I'll stay right here in the car with Bruin and keep a watch on you."

And so the three children walked slowly to the front door and Florence, being the oldest, rang the doorbell.

Henry stood behind his sister, not sure who was going to come to the door.

"What if a baddie lives here?" he asked in a worried voice and he held on to Florence's leg to give himself some courage.

A few seconds later they heard footsteps approaching the other side of the door.

The three children all took a step backwards, with Henry's fears starting to spread to the other two.

What if a man in a dirty string vest and with a face full of scars and a bristly chin answered?

But they needn't have worried and as the door

opened there was a young woman in a brightly coloured top and trousers, holding a toddler in her arms.

"Hello," she said, surprised to see three children on her doorstep and the children all relaxed.

Florence stepped forward and began to explain why they were there.

"We're sorry to trouble you but we're looking for Mrs Chisholm, who used to live here a long time ago," she said.

"Mrs Chisholm?" said the lady. "I don't know anything about her I'm afraid.

"We've only lived here for a year and we bought the house from Mr and Mrs Patel. I'm sorry but I've never heard of Mrs Chisholm."

She noticed the disappointment on the three faces in front of her and added quickly. "I tell you what, though, Mary next door has lived here for years.

"I wonder if she might know something. She's rather hard of hearing so why don't I come with you to ask her?"

"That would be very kind of you," said Harriet and the young woman stepped out of her house with her toddler still on her hip and led the children to the next door house and knocked on the door.

She had to knock again, louder this time, before the door was opened and an old lady with a woollen shawl around her shoulders and a feather duster in her hand opened the door and obviously recognised her neighbour.

"Hello Emily, how can I help you?" she asked and then tickled the toddler under her chin. "And hello Zoe. How nice to see you."

Emily stood back so she was in line with the children and told Mary: "These children are looking for someone who used to live in our house. I was wondering if you might be able to help."

"If I can," said Mary and, looking at the children, asked "so who is it you are trying to track down?

"I've lived here a long time so I might have known them." It was Harriet who stepped forward to explain things. "We're looking for Mrs Chisholm who lived here in the 1970s. Did you know her?"

"Oh, you must mean Rita. She left the street a long time ago," said Mary.

"Do you know where she went after she left?" asked Harriet hopefully.

"Oh yes, I'm still in touch with Rita. We became good friends after her husband Arthur died," said Mary.

The children couldn't hide their delight in hearing that Mary knew Mrs Chisholm. They were really getting somewhere in their investigation!

"She's not very far away. Do you want her

address?" asked Mary. "But I'd better ask why it is you want to see her, just to be on the safe side you understand."

The children could barely contain their excitement and Florence said: "We've found something that belonged to Mrs Chisholm and want to give it back.

"It would be fantastic if you could tell us where she is. We'd love to speak to her."

"Oh, how exciting. Hang on a minute," said Mary as she went back inside her house.

Emily was very happy for the children and told them: "Well, it looks like things are going well. It's time for Zoe's afternoon sleep so we'll go back inside and leave you with Mary. Good luck!"

"Thank you. You've been very kind and a great help," said Harriet and the others added their thanks as Emily went back into her house, with Zoe yawning and ready for a sleep.

Two minutes later Mary came back to the door. "I hope you don't mind but I've given Rita a ring to ask if it's ok to give you her address.

"I told her you seem very nice children and she said it would be fine. She's quite excited and wondering what it is you've found," said Mary.

"But she has to go out this afternoon and asked if you could go there tomorrow morning, at about 11."

"That will be fine. We're very excited too and

can't wait to meet Mrs Chisholm," said Florence.

Mary handed over a piece of paper. On it was written "Rita, 22 Radcliffe Road" and a telephone number.

"That's brilliant," said Harriet and she looked over her shoulder to see her mother watching from the car.

She signalled for her mother to join them and a few seconds later Mrs Wilkie and Bruin had joined the children and Mary.

"This is our mum. She'll take us to Mrs Chisholm's house tomorrow," said Harriet and Mrs Wilkie reassured Mary that the children had some good news for Mrs Chisholm.

"Well, you seem like a lovely family so I don't have any worries about giving you Rita's address," Mary said.

Mrs Wilkie and the children thanked her again and headed back to the car with Bruin.

"It seems like you're really getting somewhere. Tomorrow is going to be an exciting day," said Mrs Wilkie as the family set off for home,

That evening the children found it difficult to settle down, with thoughts of seeing Mrs Chisholm and giving back the box and all its contents of treasure.

Florence thought that, as the oldest, it was her job to try to keep everyone calm and get a good night's sleep. But it was impossible and two hours after being sent to bed, Henry was in his pyjamas and coming into the girls' bedroom.

"I can't get to sleep. I'm too excited," he told his sisters. "What do you think Mrs Chisholm will say when we see her?"

"I think she'll be very pleased to get everything back. It's going to be a big day," said Florence and she reached under her bed and pulled out the box.

She gently laid all the items side by side on the carpet and the diamond and sapphire ring sparkled again as it caught the light from the hall outside.

The three children sat in silence for several minutes looking at the treasure until Florence picked up the pieces one by one and put them back into the metal box.

"Come on," she said. "We all need to get some sleep." She took Henry by the hand and led him back to his bedroom and tucked him in.

"Goodnight little brother. Get some sleep now," she said and Henry whispered "Goodnight big sister," and closed his eyes tight and decided to do his best to go to sleep.

Ten minutes later Florence poked her head around Henry's door and saw him fast asleep and a few minutes after that she and Harriet were also asleep. It was going to be a big day and all three really needed a good night's sleep to prepare for it!

10

Mrs Chisholm's House

It wasn't long after 7am before the children started to stir.

First, as always, was Henry who lay in his bed staring at the ceiling until he thought it was all right to go into the girls' bedroom.

The time on Henry's dinosaur clock showed it was 7.13 and to Henry's delight Florence and Harriet were both awake and talking excitedly about the day ahead.

"We'll go up to the door together but I think I should do the talking and explain to Mrs Chisholm what we've found," Florence told the other two.

"Can I hold the box?" asked Henry but it was decided that as Harriet had been the one using the metal detector when the box was found she should really be the one who presents it to Mrs Chisholm.

Henry, it was decided, would be holding on to Bruin and could explain his part in digging for the box.

“Do you think we’ll get a reward?” Henry asked hopefully but was told by Florence that their reward would be seeing the pleasure in Mrs Chisholm’s face.

“Doesn’t sound much of a reward. That won’t buy a new Playstation game or even some sweets,” Henry grumbled.

But deep down he knew that giving the box back would be so exciting it didn’t really need a reward.

By 8 o’clock the children were at the breakfast table and tucking into bowls of cereal.

Usually during the summer holidays only Henry would be down that early. Harriet would follow soon afterwards but Florence would be in bed till ordered out by her mum.

But today they were all up and dressed and ready to go out before Mrs Wilkie was even out of bed.

That meant a long wait because they weren’t going anywhere until their mum was ready to take them for their 11am appointment at Mrs Chisholm’s house.

Bruin lay in his bed, keeping an eye on the children to make sure he wouldn’t be missing out on anything but happy to stay curled up until it was time to get going.

He could tell the children were very excited but was glad Mrs Wilkie was making them wait until it was time to go.

"More time for me to doze," thought Bruin who was always happy to have some extra time in bed resting.

Any thoughts of wanting to be a police dog were long gone and Bruin couldn't be happier than living with this lovely family.

As he lay there, Mr Wilkie came into the kitchen for breakfast before going off to work.

"Have a great day," he told the children as he left. "I can't wait to hear how it goes."

"We'll tell you all about it," Harriet assured him.

She had brought the box downstairs and opened the lid to look again at the treasures inside.

"I still can't believe we found this. We'll have to tell Mr Tucker at his treasure shop about it so he can tell other customers," she said.

The children sat quietly, all staring at the box of treasure until Mrs Wilkie came downstairs.

She put the box to one side as she cleared the table, telling the children to go into the sitting room and play a game until it was time to go.

They sat on the carpet and brought out a game of Snakes and Ladders but their hearts weren't in it and even when they climbed a long ladder or slid down a giant snake they weren't greeting it with the usual delight or disappointment.

An hour later it was finally time to go and the three of them leapt to their feet full of enthusiasm for the job of going to Mrs Chisholm's house.

Bruin climbed out of his bed and stood beside Henry, who had hold of his lead, and the little party headed outside and to their mum's car.

It took 15 minutes to get to Radcliffe Road and they drove slowly until spotting number 22, where Mrs Chisholm lived.

"I'll stay in the car while you go and hand over the box," Mrs Wilkie said.

The children felt a mixture of excitement and nerves, knowing they were only minutes away from handing the box over.

They climbed out of the car and walked towards the front door of number 22 and Bruin jumped out to go with them.

Did he sense somehow that he would be needed?

He walked beside the children as they made their way to Mrs Chisholm's house.

"Right, let me do the talking but you can ring the bell, Henry," said Florence.

Harriet stood holding the box, shifting nervously from one foot to the other as Henry stepped forward and rung the bell.

The children stood waiting for the door to open but after a minute it was still firmly shut.

"Ring it again," said Florence and Henry again pressed the bell, this time for longer.

Another minute and still nothing and Florence checked her watch.

It was two minutes past 11, exactly the time they had been asked to call and she wondered why Mrs Chisholm hadn't answered.

Was something wrong?

Suddenly Bruin broke away from the little group as Florence and Harriet both shouted at him to come back.

He took no notice and instead went to an open window and stood on his back legs, with his paws on the window cill.

All three children shouted at Bruin to come back but he ignored them. And then, instead of coming back as he was ordered, he leapt through the open window and into the house!

"Oh no," cried out Harriet. "What's he doing? What a naughty boy."

The children started to panic and ran to the window, shouting at Bruin to come back but he was nowhere to be seen.

"Where's he gone?" asked Henry, but no-one knew.

...instead of coming back as he was ordered, Bruin leapt through the open window and into the house!

Then, just as suddenly as he had gone, Bruin came back to the window from inside and stood barking loudly.

"What's the matter with Bruin?" Harriet asked and then ordered him to get out of the house.

"Come here Bruin, come here now!" she told him.

But Bruin took no notice and instead barked again before turning and running back through the house.

A second later he was gone but the children could hear him barking loudly from another room in the house.

"Bruin, Bruin, come here," shouted Florence but he didn't return and they could hear him still barking loudly.

"Something's wrong. Bruin's must be trying to tell us something,"

Florence said. "I'm going to go inside."

"You can't," said Harriet. "People will think you're a burglar."

But, just as Bruin had ignored them, this time it was Florence who wasn't listening. "I need to go in and see what's happened. Here, give me a leg up," she said to Harriet as they stood in front of the open window.

By now several people had been alerted to the commotion and a small crowd had started to gather outside the house.

“What’s going on?” asked a woman and another woman told her: “this girl is going to climb through the window. She thinks something is wrong. Oh, what if something’s happened to poor Rita?”

Mrs Wilkie had noticed the frantic activity and she joined the children just as Florence was disappearing inside the window.

“What are you doing Florence? Get back here at once!” she called to her daughter.

But Harriet told her “we think something is wrong. Bruin has gone in and is barking to raise the alarm.”

From outside they could hear Bruin barking as Florence disappeared head first inside the window, with her feet trailing behind as she slid to the floor.

“Are you alright Florence? Mrs Wilkie asked, her concern clear in her voice.

Two second later Florence popped up and reassured her mother: “I’m fine, I’m going to see what Bruin is barking about,” she said.

The first woman outside asked her friend: “what did she say?” and her friend replied: “she’s going inside. What a brave girl!”

Henry heard her and said proudly: “She’s my sister. She is very brave.”

As the crowd peered in through the window they

saw Florence disappear deeper into the house and could hear Bruin still barking.

"I'm going to find Bruin and see what is happening," said Florence over her shoulder as she disappeared.

"What's going on now?" asked the first woman and her friend explained that the girl was going to find her dog.

The first woman put her hand to her mouth with a worried expression. "Oh dear, I hope everything is alright," she said.

The crowd fell silent as everyone strained their ears to get any clues about what was going on and there was a murmur as Bruin suddenly stopped barking.

A few seconds later Florence came running back to the window. "It's Mrs Chisholm. She's fallen down," she said between pants.

"Is she alright?" asked the second woman.

"I don't know," said Florence. "She's unconscious. Can somebody call for an ambulance."

"I'm doing that already," said Mrs Wilkie and she spoke into her mobile phone asking for an ambulance to come to 22 Radcliffe Road.

"They'll be here as soon as they can," said Mrs Wilkie and she then told Florence: "Come and open the front door to let me in."

Florence did as she was told and a few seconds

later she was preparing to lead Mrs Wilkie to where Mrs Chisholm was lying after her fall.

"I'll come with you," said a grey haired man wearing a suit, who was in the small crowd outside the house. "My name is Dr

Jackson. I'm Mrs Chisholm's doctor."

And so the three of them were soon walking through the house to where Bruin was still standing guard over Mrs Chisholm.

Dr Jackson crouched down and lifted Mrs Chisholm's eyelids and shone a small torch into her eyes.

He turned to Florence and her mother and told them, "She's still unconscious but she's breathing and I'm sure she'll be fine.

We'll just make her comfortable and wait for the ambulance."

He turned to Florence. "It's a good job you found her. Who knows how long she would have been here otherwise," he told her.

"It wasn't me," said Florence. "It was Bruin. He knew something was wrong."

She crouched down and threw her arms around Bruin's neck.

"You're such a clever boy," she told him and the doctor agreed. "Yes, well done Bruin. You've really saved the day," he said.

Just at that point there was a rumpus in the hallway as the ambulance crew arrived and two paramedics in their green uniforms took over caring for Mrs Chisholm.

After ensuring she was not in danger, they put her on a stretcher to take her into the ambulance waiting outside.

As she was being taken out she started to recover and asked one of the ambulancemen, "what's happened, where am I?" "You're alright," the ambulanceman told her. "You've had a fall and we're taking you to hospital."

The doctor said he would go with Mrs Chisholm and he held her hand as he told her, "we're very lucky that this dog and this little girl found you," pointing to Bruin and Florence.

Mrs Chisholm looked at them. "Thank you, thank you so very much," she said quietly before she was wheeled on her stretcher out of the house.

As she went past the small crowd outside, people gasped to see their friend on a stretcher.

"Oh, poor Rita," said the first woman. "Is she going to be alright?"

One of the ambulancemen turned to tell her: "We're sure she'll be fine. We're just taking her to hospital to be checked out."

A few seconds later Mrs Wilkie, Florence and

Bruin reappeared from inside the house and there was a round of applause as they reached the crowd of people.

11

What Now? Wonder The Children

The children, their mother and Bruin stood outside the front door of number 22 as Mrs Chisholm was gently put into the back of the ambulance.

Dr Jackson came over to the family before joining her in the ambulance.

"If you give me your details I'll make sure you know how things go with Mrs Chisholm," he said kindly and Mrs Wilkie wrote down the family's telephone number and passed it over.

"I hope Mrs Chisholm is going to be ok. We've never met her before but we would really like to know how things turn out," Mrs Wilkie told the kind looking doctor.

He promised to keep them informed and then climbed into the ambulance so he could sit beside Mrs Chisholm.

The rear doors to the ambulance were then closed and, with its blue light flashing, it drove off to the hospital.

Florence and Mrs Wilkie explained to Harriet and Henry what had gone on inside the house as they crossed the road and climbed back into the car.

"But I've still got the box. What are we going to do with it now?" asked Harriet.

"Well, we'll just have to see how things turn out and wait for another opportunity to hand the box over," said Mrs Wilkie.

"For now the main thing is that Mrs Chisholm has been taken to hospital and can start the job of getting better," she told the children.

Florence said: "I don't know how Bruin knew something was wrong but he clearly did."

"Yes, it was incredible," said Harriet.

"We didn't know why Mrs Chisholm hadn't answered the door when suddenly Bruin ran off and jumped through the open window.

"He must have sensed that something was wrong," said Florence.

"And you were very brave following him," Mrs Wilkie told Florence.

Just at that moment there was a knock at the car window and as Mrs Wilkie put the window down the two ladies who had been so concerned started to speak.

"Is Rita alright?" asked the first woman. "Was she badly hurt?" asked the other.

"I'll let Florence tell you all about it," said Mrs Wilkie and Florence gave them all the details of what had happened.

"Oh my word!" said the first woman.

"Thank goodness you and your dog were here," said the second woman.

"Poor Rita could have lain there injured for hours. Goodness knows what could have happened. I hope you'll be able to see her once she gets better."

With that Mrs Wilkie explained that she ought to take the children home and they drove away with the two women and others who had gathered outside waving to them as they left.

When they reached home, the children were given glasses of strawberry milkshake as they settled down after all the excitement.

"Do you think we'll be able to see Mrs Chisholm. I do hope she's alright and we can visit her," said Harriet.

She was still holding tight on to the box as she drank her milkshake and ate three of the chocolate biscuits which Mrs Wilkie had put before them.

"I'm sure you'll be able to visit just as soon as Mrs Chisholm feels better, " Mrs Wilkie said,

"The doctor has promised to keep us in touch and there is nothing more we can do until we hear from him," she told Harriet.

The children sat quietly through their lunch and then played some Top Trumps, waiting to hear news. But there was no phone call so they had a game of Operation as the afternoon wore on, still without any news from the hospital.

Their father returned home while they were watching TV and they excitedly told him about everything that had happened.

"Well I never. What a day!" said Mr Wilkie as he helped prepare the evening meal of spaghetti Bolognese for all of them.

The family had just sat down for their meal when the telephone rang in the hallway and Mrs Wilkie went to answer it.

She thought it was either her sister calling for a chat or maybe an order for one of the wedding or birthday cakes that she made.

The children had no interest in who it was until they overheard her say: "Well, that is good news. Has she been able to say how she came to fall?"

She was obviously talking about Mrs Chisholm and a second later the children had all left the table and were gathered around their mother as she continued with the call.

They heard her say: "can you hold on for just a

minute? I must tell the children the news."

After getting a reply she put her hand over the telephone mouthpiece and told the children in a hushed voice: "It's Dr Jackson. He says Mrs Chisholm is feeling a lot better and we can go and visit her tomorrow."

The children could hardly contain their excitement and as Mrs Wilkie finished the call she and the children all went back to the dining table.

"That's brilliant news," said Harriet. "Does the doctor know what happened?"

"According to the doctor, Mrs Chisholm says she was standing on a chair looking for something in a high up cupboard when she slipped off and fell," said Mrs Wilkie.

"She knows she was very silly to do that when she was all alone in the house.

"She has a nasty sprain to her shoulder and a bad headache after knocking herself out but otherwise is fine. We'll find out more when we go to visit her tomorrow."

The children's excitement at seeing Mrs Chisholm and handing over the box quickly returned.

The job of returning the box was turning into even more of an adventure than expected and when they went to bed that night they again had difficulty getting to sleep.

Henry tried counting sheep jumping over a fence

to see if that sent him to sleep but it didn't work.

Eventually his mum popped her head around the door. She had brought up a glass of warm milk and gave it to Henry.

"This will help you get to sleep after all the excitement of the day," she told him.

Henry was starting to feel sleepy already and after drinking his milk he finally nodded off.

12

Off to The Hospital

The next morning the children were again up and dressed before eight o'clock.

But they were disappointed when their mother told them visiting hours were not until 2pm, which meant another long wait until they could leave for the hospital.

They decided to take Bruin for a walk to help pass the time and headed into the park with him.

They had brought their frisbee and Bruin had his favourite game of trying to catch the flying disc as it was thrown from one child to the other.

They were on about their tenth game when a group of older boys walked by and started shouting and laughing.

Henry had hold of the frisbee and sent it spinning towards Harriet but a gust of wind took it off course and it landed at the feet of the biggest boy in the group.

He immediately picked it up and when Henry asked for it back he said "no chance," and instead threw it to one of the other boys.

He grabbed it and sent it spinning back towards the biggest boy, who looked like the leader of the gang.

Florence politely asked him to give the frisbee back but the boy just laughed at her and started walking away. "We'll play with this later," he shouted at the children.

The rest of his gang joined him in laughing but they hadn't noticed that Bruin was looking at them and certainly didn't know that he was bred to be a police dog and that made him a very special dog indeed!

As the boys walked away Bruin came out from behind the children and ran after the leader of the gang, who still had hold of the frisbee.

When he reached him Bruin stood in front of the boy and growled. Suddenly the bully wasn't so tough and he started to whimper as Bruin stood his ground.

"Ok, ok, you can have it back. Just tell your dog to leave me alone," he said in a shaky voice.

Florence stepped forward and called to Bruin, who came straight back to her.

She held out her hand and said to the boy, "you can give it back now."

With Bruin out of the way, the boy again tried to act tough.

"Ha, I was just kidding. We're not giving it back," he said with a sneer.

Bruin heard him and stepped out from behind Florence and growled.

That was enough to make the boy think again. "Here it is," he said in a timid voice as he handed the frisbee back to Bruin.

"And don't even think about taking it again!" shouted Henry bravely as the older boys retreated, still frightened by Bruin.

"Well, that's them sorted out," said Florence as the gang disappeared. She looked at her watch and saw it was one o'clock – time to get back for a quick lunch before going to the hospital.

After a bowl of tomato soup and some bread and butter it was time to leave for the hospital and they got there just after 2pm.

Bruin was left in the car with the windows open and under the shade of a tree as they went to reception and were directed to Myrtle Ward, where Mrs Chisholm was in a bed.

Harriet was holding on to the box and all three children were nervous as they stood in the lift to take them to the ward.

That was enough to make the boy think again. "Here it is," he said in a timid voice as he handed the frisbee back to Bruin

As they emerged they saw the rows of beds and Mrs Wilkie asked a nurse where they could find Mrs Chisholm.

Seconds later the children were around the bed of Mrs Chisholm and the old lady put on her glasses so she could see them properly.

She assured them she was feeling a lot better and would be going home the next day. "I was just trying to reach a vase for some flowers when I fell. I won't be doing that again," she told them.

"But why were you at my house? Mary said you had found something that belonged to me," Mrs Chisholm said.

Harriet stepped forward with the box.

"Do you recognise this?" she asked and Mrs Chisholm's face immediately brightened up.

"My word, I haven't seen that box for years and years. I can't believe it's here, on my bed," she told the children.

Florence laid the box on Mrs Chisholm's bed and gently lifted the lid.

One by one she put the treasures on to the blanket and Mrs Chisholm's eyes began to mist with tears as she saw the cufflinks, the pen, the photograph, the pearls and the silver coins.

Finally Florence unwrapped the diamond and sapphire ring and Mrs Chisholm gasped, putting her hand to her mouth as she saw it.

The tears fell down her cheek as she picked up the ring.

"I don't believe it. I never expected to see this again," she said.

She then told the children and Mrs Wilkie a story which made them go silent and all stood close to tears as the tale unfolded.

"This was my engagement ring from Arthur. It went missing in the late 1970s and Arthur was convinced that Matthew, our son, had stolen it and sold it.

"There was a terrible row and Matthew insisted he hadn't touched it.

"But Arthur refused to believe him and Matthew stormed out of the house, slamming the front door as he left.

"That was over 40 years ago I haven't seen Matthew or heard from him to this day. I have no idea where he is.

"He was 17 years old and we reported him missing to the police but have never had any news.

"I miss Matthew terribly and never a day goes by when I don't think about him and wonder how he is.

"And to think, the ring was in the box all the time. I can hardly believe it," Mrs Chisholm said.

She explained that her husband had hidden the box after they had a burglary but he became very forgetful and couldn't remember where he had buried it or what was inside it. "He forgot the ring was in there and blamed Matthew instead. What a dreadful thing," Mrs Chisholm said between sobs.

"Poor Matthew getting the blame when he was completely innocent, just like he always insisted."

The children and Mrs Wilkie stood frozen to the spot as they heard the story.

Mrs Chisholm put the ring and all the other items back into the box. "This is such an important box and I don't feel it would be safe just left here beside my bed. I don't ever want to lose it again," Mrs Chisholm said.

"Would you take it back with you and then perhaps bring it to me after I go home?" she asked the children and they said they would gladly look after it.

They told Mrs Chisholm how they had found it and about Bruin jumping through her open window after she had had her fall.

"My word, I have so much to thank you all for. And Bruin of course. Perhaps I can meet him when you bring the box back to me," Mrs Chisholm said, her eyes still misty with tears.

Harriet said: "We'll make sure to bring Bruin with us. He would love to see you again as well, and make sure you're ok I'm sure."

The story of the box and about Matthew had shocked the children and their mother and the joy they thought they would feel at handing the box back was replaced by a deep sorrow at the sad story.

They all had their heads bowed as they walked back to the car park in silence, with Florence holding on tightly to the box of treasure.

Bruin was waiting patiently for them as they climbed back into the car and Florence was the one to break the silence. "Our job is only half done," she said.

"What do you mean?" asked Harriet.

"We've shown Mrs Chisholm the box but now we need to find Matthew and tell him the ring has been found," said Florence.

"But how will we do that?" asked Henry.

"I don't know. But we must do it," said Florence with determination in her voice.

"Yes, we must," agreed Harriet. "I can't believe Matthew has been missing for all these years. And all because of something he hadn't done."

The children were driven home by Mrs Wilkie, with the three of them starting to think of ways to find Matthew but they couldn't come up with any ideas.

When they returned home their father was already there, waiting to hear what he expected to be a happy story about the box being given back.

But when he was told about the ring Mr Wilkie fell silent. The children though were already working on a plan for stage two of their job!

13

Can Matthew Be Found?

As the family sat around the kitchen table they began work on what they called "Operation Find Matthew," and started simply with an internet search under the name Matthew Chisholm.

This revealed an actor under that name and a host of businessmen but it was impossible to know if any of them was the Matthew Chisholm they were looking for.

It was Mr Wilkie who said: "I think we should ask Tingleside Police for help. I'm sure they will want to help once we explain that we are Bruin's new owners."

Mrs Wilkie agreed and said the first thing they should do was to get hold of Mrs Green and her daughter, Jasmine.

They had been the puppy walkers for Bruin before it was decided he wouldn't make it as a police dog.

"We could ask if they had any contacts in the Tingleside police," said Mrs Wilkie and without hesitation she looked up their telephone number and rang them.

Two minutes later she was back in the kitchen to report that Mrs Green and Jasmine would be coming over that afternoon to see if they could help.

"They were very excited he hear how Bruin is getting on and can't wait to see him," said Mrs Wilkie to the children.

"I don't think there's anything else we can do until we see them. Why don't you take Bruin out for a walk while we're waiting?" Mr Wilkie told the children and they agreed that would be the best idea.

They put Bruin on his lead and he followed the children out of the house and past their neighbour, Mr Hedges, who was in his garden trying to shoo away a family of seagulls sitting on his car.

"I don't know what they want," Mr Hedges told the children as they walked past.

He didn't like the seagulls and had a number of things to try to put them off, including a remote control plastic hawk which flapped its wings and squawked whenever a seagull went near.

But the gulls had worked out that it wasn't a real hawk and ignored it. One of them even sat on the hawk's head!

What Mr Hedges didn't know was that as soon as he went out, every day his wife would sneak into the garden and feed scraps to the family of seagulls so that was why they were always hanging around.

If Mrs Hedges ever saw any of the children as she was feeding the birds she would put a finger to her lips and whisper "sshh" to make sure they never told her husband what she was doing.

They agreed to keep quiet and as Mr Hedges scratched his head, wondering why the birds were still there, the children just shrugged their shoulders in a "search me" sort of way without revealing the secret.

They took Bruin around the block, talking about the seagulls and about whether they would find Matthew Chisholm to tell him the engagement ring had been found.

"We must do our best," said Florence and the others agreed they would do all they could.

When they got back to the house they were given milk and biscuits and settled in the sitting room to wait for Mrs Green and Jasmine.

So much had happened since that afternoon when they first heard about the children in

Spain who had found the Roman coins and then decided to become treasure hunters themselves. Now they just hoped they could somehow find the missing Matthew.

But how would they do it? It was such a long time since Matthew had disappeared.

Florence was lost in her thoughts, wondering if the Tingleside police would help them, when there was a ring on the doorbell and the children raced to the front door, where their mother was already letting Mrs Green and Jasmine in.

"Where's Bruin?" Jasmine asked straight away and, on hearing his name, the big friendly dog climbed out of his bed and came into the hall.

Mrs Green and her daughter both ran to him and threw their arms around his neck and Bruin clearly remembered them straight away and gave them both friendly licks to show how pleased he was to see them.

"My, how he's grown," said Mrs Green. "And still as soft and gentle as ever. Bruin has found his purpose in life, and it's not as a police dog!"

Mrs Wilkie was quick to tell Mrs Green and Jasmine that although he did not want to be a police dog, Bruin had put his training to good use.

She told them about Bruin finding Mrs Chisholm after her fall and about an earlier incident when he tracked down Henry after he had wandered off and slipped down a steep bank and was unable to get back up.

"Oh, you clever boy," said Jasmine, giving Bruin an extra hug and she followed the German Shepherd into the sitting room to be with Florence, Harriet and Henry.

"It looks like Bruin has really settled in," said Jasmine and Harriet was first to agree.

"He loves living here and we love having him here," she told Jasmine.

It was then that she noticed a sad look and a tear in Jasmine's eyes. "What's the matter Jasmine?" she asked.

"Oh, nothing. I'm just being silly," Jasmine told Harriet. But the children weren't going to leave it at that.

"Come on Jasmine, we can see something is wrong, what is it?" asked Florence.

Jasmine was clearly upset about something, so Harriet asked again: "Come on Jasmine, tell us what's wrong."

"I'm just being silly," said Jasmine again.

But as she stroked Bruin and gently rubbed his ears, more tears began to well up in her eyes.

Florence went to sit next to her on the sofa and placed her hand on Jasmine's to give her reassurance and asked again what was wrong.

It was then that Jasmine said: "It's just that my mum has a new job, as a carer at the old folks home."

"Well, that's good isn't it?" asked Harriet.

"It would be, but it means we can't have puppies any longer for the police. I'm already missing them terribly.

"Bruin will be the last one we ever looked after. It's just made me so sad to see him again and think we'll never have any more like him.

"He was the kindest, cuddliest dog we ever looked after," Jasmine said.

"Well, we love him to bits so thank you for letting him come to live with us here," Florence said gently.

Then Harriet came up with an idea. "Why don't you come round and join us on walks with Bruin. I'm sure he'd love that," she said.

"Are you sure?" said Jasmine, her face brightening up at the thought of seeing more of Bruin.

"Of course we're sure," said Harriet. And Florence quickly added: "That would be great and if we go away on holiday maybe you could look after Bruin for us!"

"That would be fantastic. I feel so much better already," said Jasmine

So it was agreed that Jasmine would see much more of Bruin, starting with today!

They would set off straight away on their first walk, through the park and down by the river which ran through Tingleside and into the sea.

They told their mothers where they were going and, putting Bruin on his lead, headed out of the house, the four of them all in a good mood and happy to be together.

As they left the garden they spotted Mr Hedges next door. He had clearly just washed his car and was trying to scare away two seagulls and their youngster, which still had its grey feathers.

The birds were standing on the roof of the sparkling vehicle.

He was clapping his hands and waving his arms but the seagulls were going nowhere – little did Mr Hedges know that as soon as he was gone Mrs Hedges would be out with the latest feast of scraps for them.

"Those seagulls still a nuisance I see Mr Hedges," said Florence as they passed his gate.

"I don't know why they've picked on my car to be the one to sit on all day. I've just spent an hour cleaning it and now they're going to make it mucky again," he complained.

The children kept the secret about his wife feeding the birds and, once out of sight, Florence giggled as she explained to Jasmine about the seagulls next door.

"But you mustn't ever tell Mr Hedges about what happens as soon as he goes out," she said.

"No, I won't say anything," said Jasmine, chuckling, and with her arms swinging by her side she set off with her new friends, feeling a hundred times better!

14

Excitement on The Walk

Harriet was holding on to Bruin's lead as the small group used the zebra crossing to get to the park and Bruin was clearly enjoying being out with everyone.

He trotted along with his head held high, keeping a close eye on everything that was going on and every now and again Jasmine would put out her hand to stroke him or pat his head.

"He's such a good boy, not pulling hard on the lead or getting under everyone's feet," said Jasmine in admiration.

The girls and Henry were quick to agree that Bruin was indeed a very good boy.

The little group entered the park and Henry ran ahead for a go on the swings, while the girls chatted about the summer holidays and what they had been up to, as they began getting used to becoming good friends.

After five minutes on the swings, Henry was told to join the others and they set off to the edge of the park.

They headed towards the river bank, with Bruin trusted to walk with them without his lead.

Ahead of them was another group of three girls, two of them chatting together and one of the girls on her mobile phone. It was a lovely, sunny day with hardly a cloud in the sky.

Suddenly there was a whooshing sound as a boy on a bike whizzed past Bruin and the children and toward the other three youngsters.

As he approached them he slowed down slightly and aimed his bike so that he was between the two who were chatting and their friend, talking on her mobile.

What happened next only took a second and took everyone by surprise.

As the boy on the bike went past the group of three friends he put out his hand and snatched away the mobile phone before peddling hard to get away.

"Hey. That's my phone!" the girl shouted as the boy raced away, standing out of the saddle to get more speed.

"I don't believe it, he's stolen her mobile," said Jasmine in shock.

The four of them stood open mouthed, hardly

believing what they had just seen but Bruin wasn't frozen to the spot like they were!

The black and tan German Shepherd quickly broke into a run and chased after the thief, who by now was close to the edge of the park.

"Bruin, Bruin, get back here," shouted Florence and Harriet but Bruin took no notice and carried on running after the boy on his bike.

A few seconds later he was out of the park and the group could hear Bruin barking as he ran after the thief.

It only took a minute for Bruin to get alongside the boy.

He barked and growled as he ran next to the bike on the path that ran beside the river.

The three girls and Henry ran out of the park and could see Bruin and the boy on the bike.

The thief was being forced towards the river as Bruin chased alongside, barking louder and louder, and he had to slow down as Bruin came closer and closer.

At the end of the path there was nowhere for the thief to go and he steered his bike off the path and on to the soft grass.

The change of surface meant the bike wobbled out of control and the boy fell off, sliding down the muddy bank and straight into the river!

He dropped the stolen phone as he slid and with

a great splash went into the river and was quickly up to his neck in the cold water.

"Help, help, I can't swim," he shouted as the current of the river began to drag him away from the bank.

Two men who were sitting on stools fishing in the river pointed at the boy but were too shocked and worried about the danger of the river to do anything.

Bruin though didn't think about the danger and was quickly down the bank and into the river.

The thief was panicking and flapping his arms as he continued to shout for help and twice his head dipped under the water and he came back up gasping for air.

Bruin swam out to the boy and grabbed hold of his jacket with his teeth and, swimming as hard as he could, dragged him back to dry land.

Panting hard, the boy crawled out of the river and up the muddy bank where he lay on his back, totally exhausted.

Bruin also clambered out of the river and up the bank and shook himself to get rid of some of the water in his coat.

By now both groups of children had caught up and the stolen mobile phone was spotted lying in the grass where the thief had dropped it.

Harriet picked it up and handed it back to its grateful owner.

"Thank you," the girl said. "I was only given the phone for my birthday last week. I can't believe what has happened. Your dog is a hero!"

Both groups of children gathered around Bruin and Jasmine took off her jacket to rub Bruin's coat and help get him dry.

"What a star you are, Bruin. Goodness me!" she was telling him.

Just at that moment there was the voice of a man, standing behind the children.

"Hello, hello, hello. What's been going on here then? Why did your dog chase this boy?" the tall man asked.

They explained that the boy had snatched the phone and Bruin had chased after him.

The man told them he was an off-duty policeman who was on his way to Tingleside station. He stood over the soaking wet thief and told him to get to his feet.

The boy stood up, his face fixed in an ugly scowl as the policeman ordered him to give his name, address and age.

It turned out he was 15 years old and lived close to the park.

"Right, I think a visit to your parents is in order," the policeman told him and he held on to the sullen boy as he ordered him to pick up his bike and they walked off towards the boy's nearby house.

Bruin swam out to the boy and grabbed hold of his jacket with his teeth and, swimming as hard as he could, dragged him back to dry land.

But before they left, the policeman got the details of the owner of the phone and of Bruin and the other children.

"Bruin?" he said as he was told the dog's name.

"I knew a Bruin. He was bred to be a police dog but didn't make it and went to live with a family," the policeman said.

"This is him," said Florence proudly. "He's our dog and he is the loveliest and bravest animal in the world ever!"

The girl who owned the mobile phone stepped forward and gave Bruin a hug. "He certainly is the best ever. Thank you Bruin, you're a real star," she said.

The policeman agreed. "My name is PC Harper and I'll be in touch to let you know what has happened to this lad," he said pointing to the young thief.

As they walked off towards the boy's home the others said their goodbyes and the three girls went off to the shops as Florence, Harriet, Henry, Bruin and Jasmine turned and headed back to the house.

As they walked past their neighbours' house, Mr Hedges had gone out in his car and Mrs Hedges was sitting on the bench in the front garden.

The two adult seagulls and their youngster were standing at her feet happily pecking at the scraps of food she was dropping for them.

She smiled at the children as they walked past and they waved to her, with Henry putting his finger to his lips to show that her secret was safe with them.

They entered the house while Mrs Wilkie and Mrs Green were enjoying a cup of coffee after working on a plan to try to find Mrs Chisholm's son, even though it was over 40 years since he had gone missing.

"Have you had a nice time?" Mrs Wilkie asked, having no idea of the drama of the stolen phone and Bruin's part in getting it back and catching the thief.

"Well, where do we start?" said Jasmine.

"That sounds interesting. Has there been some excitement?" asked Mrs Green and the children all started talking at once to tell the story.

"One at a time!" said Mrs Wilkie and she asked Jasmine to explain everything and she told the whole story.

"So Bruin was a real hero?" asked Mrs Green. "I'll come through to the sitting room so I can say well done."

But Bruin hadn't gone through to the sitting room. Instead he was curled up in his bed, happily dozing.

"Typical Bruin, he'll never change," said Mrs Green fondly as she looked lovingly at Bruin.

15

Find Matthew

Mrs Green and Mrs Wilkie had spent the time while the children were out deciding the best way to track down the missing Matthew Chisholm.

It was many years since he had left the family home after being accused of stealing the engagement ring and no-one had heard of him since then.

Mrs Wilkie had hoped Mrs Green's connection with the Tingleside police would mean they could help track him down.

But Mrs Green explained that she was no longer involved with the puppy walking for the police and that officially they would not be able to do much to help.

"The only thing I can think of is making an

appeal on Facebook, asking if anyone knows where Matthew is these days," she had said.

It seemed a shame that the police would not be able to help officially and plans were made to put an appeal on Facebook.

Just then the doorbell rang and Harriet answered the door, to see PC Harper standing on the doorstep.

"Hello again," he said. "I thought I'd come round and let you know how things went with the lad who stole the mobile phone."

"Oh, thanks. Everyone's here," said Harriet and she invited him into the sitting room where all the others were gathered and she explained to her mum and Mrs Green about the policeman's part in the adventure.

"Yes," said PC Harper. "I took the lad back to his house and told his parents what had happened.

They were very shocked to hear what he had been up to but relieved that he had been saved from the river by Bruin. "They gave him a very severe telling off."

"Will he go to prison?" asked Henry.

"No, that won't happen.

"It's the first time he's been in trouble like this and we like to give youngsters a chance to put things right in another way," the policeman said.

He was asked to explain what he meant and he

said: "Locking up youngsters like this can lead them more onto a path of crime once they come out from jail.

"Instead we like to make them face up to what they've done and do some good for the community to make up for it.

"Sometimes they'll do work like painting walls or cleaning up litter, other times they will actually do things for their victims like some work on their house.

"In this case, I'm going to send the lad to do gardening work at the Tingleside Old Folks' home.

"He will have to go there every Saturday and Sunday for the next eight weeks so as well as being punished by not being allowed to go out with his mates, he'll do some good for the community," said PC Harper.

"Wow, what a coincidence," said Mrs Green. "That's where I've just started a new job as a carer. I'll keep an eye on him and make sure he does what he should!"

Florence was listening to all of this but at the same time was thinking up a plan.

She thought to herself "Why don't we ask this friendly policeman if he can help us to find Matthew Chisholm?"

Without discussing it with anyone else she blurted out the story of the found treasure and the need to find Mrs Chisholm's son.

"Well, I can't use the police computer to track down people unofficially I'm afraid," the policeman told Florence. But then he added: "What did you say the name was again?"

"Matthew Chisholm. He used to live in Boyle Terrace," Florence said, despite her mother trying to stop her.

"Hmmm, Matthew Chisholm. I know someone of that name who used to live in Tingleside.

"I went to school with him and still chat to him sometimes. I wonder if it's the same one?" PC Harper said.

"Give me all the details you have, like his parents' names, and I'll see what I can do.

"I won't be able to give you his address but if it turns out to be the one you're looking for I could call him and let him have your number."

"That would be fantastic," said Florence and everyone else agreed.

They gave PC Harper as much information as they could and decided not to do anything about the Facebook appeal until they had heard back from the police officer, who left the house promising to let them know how he got on.

"That sounds really encouraging," said Mrs Wilkie to the children.

"So not only has Bruin caught a thief and recovered a stolen mobile phone, he may have set us on the track to solving the mystery of Matthew Chisholm!"

Jasmine crouched down by Bruin's basket, stroking him gently and speaking quietly to the sleepy dog.

"You are such a clever boy Bruin and it's soooo good to see you again," she was saying as Florence and Harriet came and knelt beside her on the kitchen floor.

"Not every walk will be as exciting as today's but we'll always have fun. We're so glad you're going to be joining us," Florence told Jasmine.

"Yes, it's going to be lovely just joining up and coming on walks," said Jasmine, remembering how she had found a new home for Bruin by putting up a poster at school.

"I can tell Bruin is really happy here. It was a good day when you spotted that notice saying there was a dog that needed a new home!" she told Florence.

But then Mrs Green said it was time for them to go and Florence and Harriet promised to be in touch as soon as there was any news from PC Harper about finding Matthew Chisholm.

There was clearly a lot more excitement still to come!

Jasmine crouched down by Bruin's basket, stroking him gently and speaking to the sleepy dog.

News From PC Harper

It was just two days later that PC Harper rang and spoke to Mrs Wilkie.

"I've got some news for you about Matthew," the policeman told her and she asked him to hang on for a moment while she called the children to the hallway.

"I've put the phone onto loudspeaker so the children can hear the news as well," Mrs Wilkie said and PC Harper said that was fine.

"After leaving your house I got back to the station and had a few minutes before going out on patrol so I looked up Matthew's number and gave him a call.

"Unfortunately he wasn't in but I left a message asking him to ring me," the policeman reported.

The children gathered closer to the telephone to

get ready for the next piece of news.

"Have you heard anything from him?" asked Mrs Wilkie and Florence crossed her fingers as she stared nervously at the telephone.

"Yes, I'm pleased to say I heard from Matthew today," said PC Harper.

"I told him his mother had been taken into hospital and that she would love to see him.

"He was very relieved to hear she was going to be fine and he wants to come and see her.

"I also told him there were three children living here in Tingleside who had some very exciting news," PC Harper reported.

The children hung on to each other as they listened out for the next bit of information.

"I have heard from the hospital that Mrs Chisholm went home yesterday and is feeling a lot better," said PC Harper.

"I have passed your telephone number on to Matthew and perhaps you could arrange a meeting between him and Mrs Chisholm?

"It's been so many years since Matthew left that I think he is very nervous about just ringing his mother.

"it seems it would be better if you all acted as a sort of go-between to help organise the first meeting between mother and son.

"He said he would call tonight and perhaps you could arrange a time for the meeting?"

"Yes, we'll certainly do that," said Mrs Wilkie.

"We can all understand it being difficult to just pick things up after all these years and perhaps having some extra people about will help.

"Thank you PC Harper, we are all very grateful for what you've done."

The children then all shouted "Thank you PC Harper" and he told them he was very glad things looked like working out.

After the call from the policeman there was nothing the children could do but wait to hear from Matthew in the evening.

They decided to take Bruin for a walk and headed for the beach, where all the excitement had begun just a few days earlier.

"Can we take the metal detector?" asked Henry and so it was decided they would take it down with them, just in case there was something else exciting hiding under the sand.

As they walked on to the beach Bruin was allowed to run ahead and he set off along the sand, enjoying the freedom of the wide open space with Henry running behind.

Suddenly Bruin stopped, turned his head to check that the children were following, and then started furiously digging at the sand, sending it spraying behind him in a big arc.

The children ran to him and gathered around as a hole appeared. Bruin stopped digging and stuck his nose into the hole instead.

He brought his head out and whined, as if to say "there's something here," and Harriet turned the metal detector on.

"Move Bruin out of the way, I'm going to see what's there," she told the others as Henry and Florence pulled Bruin out of the way and held on to his collar.

Harriet moved forward and put the metal detector into the hole. At first there was nothing but as she moved it around there was suddenly a loud "beeeep" as the detector found something.

Florence dropped to her knees, and using the small spade which they always kept with the metal detector and the treasure bag, started digging where the beep had been heard.

"There's something here," she said excitedly as the spade clanged against something metal.

She scraped around the object, waiting to see what it was. "Is it treasure?" asked Henry as the object was slowly uncovered. He was remembering the moment when Mrs Chisholm's treasure box was found.

Florence kept digging until suddenly there it was – but it wasn't treasure. "It's an old dog food tin with some dried up food still inside it," said

Bruin started furiously digging at the sand, sending it spraying behind him in a big arc.

Florence as the rusty old tin was held up for all to see.

"No wonder Bruin was so excited but it's just more rubbish."

She pulled the tin out and put it in her bag so they could throw it away properly.

"At least that's one less piece of rubbish spoiling the beach," she said and the children all laughed and hugged Bruin.

"It's back to normal, just finding rubbish," said Harriet and the little group headed toward the sea to let Bruin have a paddle in the water before heading home

Back home was where they knew there would be some real excitement, waiting for Matthew's telephone call!

17

Will Matthew Call?

There was fish fingers, chips and peas for tea and the children ate in silence, all listening out for the telephone and the call from Matthew.

But as they finished their meal no call had been received from Mrs Chisholm's son.

"It's early still, only half past six," Mrs Wilkie told her children.

She was trying to keep their spirits up but secretly was wondering whether Matthew would call or whether too many years had passed since he had last been in touch with his mother.

The children gathered in the sitting room after tea and as the clock ticked past 7pm there was still no call.

Henry was getting particularly worried as it would be his bed time in half an hour. "Please ring, please ring," he whispered to himself but as the clock reached 7.15 there was still no call.

Then suddenly, at 7.20, the phone rang and the children ran into the hall to look eagerly at the telephone.

The message dial was reading an unfamiliar number so it wasn't nana or auntie Laura, as it often was.

Mrs Wilkie came to the telephone and the children stood back as she answered it.

"Hello, Tingleside 664432," she said before going silent as the other person spoke.

Quickly she covered the mouthpiece as she whispered to the children "it's Matthew!" before returning to the call and shooing the children into the sitting room so she could talk without any interruptions.

The children waited by the closed door between the sitting room and the hall, straining to hear what was being said but they were unable to make out anything other than a low mumble.

"We can't hear what's going on," said an annoyed Florence and she went to sit on the sofa to wait for news and a few seconds later the other two joined her while Mrs Wilkie carried on with the telephone call.

Less than a minute later the door opened and Mrs Wilkie stood before the children and saw the expectant looks in their faces.

"Well?" asked Florence, unable to wait any longer for the news.

Mrs Wilkie took another step into the sitting room and then announced: "We're going to meet Matthew at Mrs Chisholm's house tomorrow morning at 11 o'clock."

It was the news the children had desperately wanted to hear and they all let out a cheer.

Florence immediately ran to her bedroom to collect the box of treasure and brought it back to the sitting room.

She carefully laid the pieces on the carpet.

"We just need to make extra sure everything is here," she explained as she carefully lifted the pieces out of the box.

First the gold pen, then the photograph in its silver frame, then the cufflinks and the pearls followed by the silver coins. But where was the diamond and sapphire engagement ring?

Florence tipped the box upside down and shook it for 10 seconds in case the ring had become stuck but nothing appeared.

Harriet peered inside and explored the box with her hands. "Oh no! It's not here," she said.

Henry, on the other side of the coffee table in the middle of the lounge, was keeping very quiet and casually looking around him in a "search me" sort of way.

Both girls immediately became suspicious of their little brother.

"Do you know where the ring is?" asked Florence.

Henry replied "What ring?" which just made his sisters even more convinced that he had something to do with the disappearing ring.

"You know very well which ring, the one from the treasure box," said Harriet as she fixed her brother with a steely look.

Now, Henry was only six but he knew when the game was up and he quickly thought how he could get himself off.

"Oh, THAT ring," he said. "I didn't know you meant THAT ring."

"Come on," said Florence, advancing on her little brother and standing over him. "Of course we mean that ring. What have you done with it?"

Henry thought quickly how to get out of this tight corner and he told the girls "Uh, I put it in a safe place," he told them.

"It was already in a safe place," said Harriet as she went and stood next to her sister, towering over Henry with her arms crossed and a serious look on her face.

"Go and get it," she told him.

Henry scrambled to his feet and ran out of the lounge and up to his room. He reappeared a minute later with the ring.

The little boy was still feeling guilty about upsetting everyone but Bruin snuffled his nose into Henry's neck

"I just wanted to look at it but then forgot to put it back in the box," he told them.

Florence and Harriet both looked really cross but to Henry's great relief, his mother arrived in the sitting room at that moment.

After being told what had happened she said, "all's well that ends well. Now we have everything in place to take to Mrs Chisholm. No harm done."

But Florence and Harriet weren't ready to let their brother off so easily. "What if we'd got there and the ring was missing?" asked Florence.

Henry bowed his head and mumbled "sorry, I didn't mean to keep it. I just forgot to put it back in the box."

Again, his mother came to his aid and told Florence "well done for checking. Now everything is fine.

"Henry has said sorry and we have a very exciting day to look forward to," said Mrs Wilkie calmly.

Henry's sisters were still annoyed with him and weren't ready to forgive him as everything was put back into the box ready for the next day.

As everyone went quiet, thinking about tomorrow, Bruin climbed out of his bed and went across to Henry, who was close to tears.

The little boy was still feeling guilty about

upsetting everyone but Bruin snuffled his nose into Henry's neck and as Henry put his arms around the friendly dog he slowly started to feel better.

He looked across to his sisters and told them: "I'm really sorry about the ring. I won't do anything like that again."

By now they had calmed down and they both went over to their little brother and put their arms around him and around Bruin.

"Come on, let's hug it out," said Harriet and Henry knew he had finally been forgiven and they could all look forward to the next day.

Everything was in the box and Matthew had been tracked down. What a day lay ahead and Florence rang Jasmine to tell her of all the developments in the case.

18

Back To Mrs Chisholm's House

It was still dark and the house was very quiet as Henry woke up the next morning, not knowing if anyone else was awake yet.

He strained his ears for any sounds of activity but could just hear the ticking of the old clock in the hallway downstairs.

Suddenly the clock started the familiar bongs which signalled an hour and Henry counted them as they rang out. Bong, bong, bong, bong, bong, bong went the clock. Only six bongs!

It was just six o'clock and he knew his sisters wouldn't thank him if he went into their room straight away.

So again he lay as still as can be, listening out for any sounds which would indicate that Florence and Harriet were awake.

After 10 minutes of lying still, Henry couldn't wait any longer.

He knew someone who would be pleased to see him, whatever the time was and he slipped out of bed, put on his slippers and dressing gown and, quiet as a mouse, sneaked downstairs and into the kitchen.

Bruin lifted his head and wagged his tail as he heard the door open and he saw Henry tiptoe into the kitchen.

Bruin was stretched out on his bed and Henry knelt on the floor beside him and snuggled up to the sleepy dog.

He lay his head on a spare bit of Bruin's bed and wrapped an arm around the pet.

"You're my best friend, Bruin. You don't mind me coming in early," Henry whispered to him and he received a friendly lick in return.

Henry felt the warmth from Bruin and he felt happy and secure lying next to him.

He patted Bruin's shoulder and thought about the day ahead. He didn't want to close his eyes but somehow they....did.....just.....close......and then......zzzzzzz!

It was just gone 8.30 before Mrs Wilkie went down to the kitchen to make some tea and there, lying on the dog's bed fast asleep, was not only Bruin but Henry as well.

"Oh Henry, what are you doing there?" she asked and Henry stirred awake on hearing the question.

"I woke up early and decided to come down-stairs and just went to say hello to Bruin. I must have fallen asleep," the six year-old said.

"Well, you were certainly fast asleep when I came into the kitchen," said his mother.

"And Bruin's no better, look at him just lying there enjoying having his little friend cuddled up to him!"

Henry stood up as he heard the kettle come to the boil and after Mrs Wilkie poured the tea for her and Mr Wilkie she told Henry: "Come on, back upstairs. I expect Florence and Harriet are awake by now."

Henry said "OK" and trudged up the stairs behind his mother, saying "see ya later," to Bruin before peeling off at the girls' bedroom and gently knocking on the door.

"Come in," came a voice from inside and Henry slipped into the bedroom to see Florence and Harriet sitting up in their beds.

Florence had the treasure box on her lap and had checked and then double checked that everything was there.

"What time are we going?" asked Henry and he was reminded they were going to get to the house at 11.

They would be going in the car with their mother. "Can Bruin come?" asked Henry and he was told that, yes, Bruin would be coming.

Having checked that all was well in the box, Henry went off to the bathroom and then his bedroom to get dressed.

Florence closed the lid and made sure a ribbon was in place and tied tight around the box to prevent it opening by accident.

"It's a big day for us but an even bigger one for Mrs Chisholm and Matthew. They haven't seen each other for years," said Florence.

"Can you imagine that? Not seeing mummy and daddy for years," she asked.

"It would be terrible. I hope nothing ever makes that happen to us," said Harriet.

"I'm sure it won't," Florence said to reassure her younger sister.

"Come on, it's time for us to get up and have some breakfast."

Half an hour later the children were all dressed and sitting around the kitchen table, having cereal and toast for breakfast.

It was Monday morning in the second week of the school holidays and Mr Wilkie had gone to work, wishing everyone well before he left.

Bruin was given his breakfast and Mrs Wilkie, who was on a diet, just had half a grapefruit and a black coffee.

It wasn't fair that her business was making wedding cakes and birthday cakes for people but she could never eat any herself because she seemed to always be on a diet, Florence and Harriet thought.

But, unknown to her family, Mrs Wilkie had a secret store of biscuits and she sneaked one or two when no-one was watching.

She also had a secret supply of chocolates which the rest of the family knew nothing about and, again, she made sure no-one else was around when she took one!

The children all put their bowls and plates into the washing up bowl and then went into the sitting room for a game of Mousey Mousey until they were ready to leave.

Eventually their mother put her head around the door and told the children it was time to go.

They filed through the kitchen and Harriet put Bruin's lead on him.

"Come on, time to get going," she said to Bruin and he got back to his feet and stood patiently while his lead was attached.

Florence made sure she had the treasure box with her and Henry double checked the time with his mother.

"It's a quarter to eleven," she told him. "It

should only take us ten minutes at the most to get there."

The car pulled up on the opposite side of the road to Mrs Chisholm's house and less than a minute later another car came to a stop just in front of them.

"Is that Matthew?" Harriet asked as the new car parked.

"I don't know yet. Wait a minute, someone's getting out….It's a man. It must be Matthew," said Mrs Wilkie.

The man walked towards the car.

He was about the same age as the children's father and had a kind face. He was carrying a large bunch of flowers.

He stopped alongside the driver's window and Mrs Wilkie pressed the button to wind the window down.

"You must be the Wilkie family," the man said with a smile.

"Yes, we are. And you must be Matthew," said Mrs Wilkie.

"That's right. I've been away too long and it's time for me to see mum again," he said.

"We've got a treasure box which your father buried on the beach over 50 years ago," Florence told him.

"I've been told to expect a surprise but I don't know what it is. That must be it," Matthew said.

"I'm rather nervous. I've been away for such a long time.

Would you all come in with me?"

"Of course we will," said Mrs Wilkie.

"Come on children, bring the treasure box and bring Bruin as well. He's played a big part in all of this."

"That's great," said Matthew.

"And I've brought something of a surprise as well. Certainly a surprise for my mother after all these years."

He then turned towards his car and jerked his head as if to say "come on."

The front car door and both back doors opened. Out came a woman and two children, aged about 14 to 16, a boy and a girl.

They walked up to be beside Matthew. "This is my wife, Moira, and children Imary and Edward.

"They have never met their grandmother so it's a really big day for all of us," he said.

"Pleased to meet you," said Mrs Wilkie as the children lined up beside her. "This is Florence, Harriet and Henry."

"And this is Bruin. He's our dog," said Henry as

he held on to Bruin's lead.

"Right, time to go in," said Matthew and the group checked for traffic and then crossed the road to be outside Mrs Chisholm's house.

"Stand back, children. Let Matthew and his family go first," said Mrs Wilkie and the children and Bruin stood aside as Matthew, Moira, Imary and Edward went to the door and Matthew rang the bell.

Almost instantly the door was opened and Mrs Chisholm stood there.

"Oh Matthew. I can't believe it," she said as she looked at the son she last saw then he was 17 years old.

"Hello mum. These are for you," Matthew said as he passed over the flowers. There was a tear in his eyes.

He noticed his mother looking at the others standing just behind him.

Matthew stood aside and forward walked his wife and two children. "This is Moira, my wife and your daughter in law," he said and Moira stepped forward.

Mrs Chisholm immediately gave her a hug before letting go and looking at her two children.

"And this is Imary and Edward, your grandchildren," said Moira and Mrs Chisholm had tears running down her cheeks.

"I don't believe it. A daughter in law and grandchildren I knew nothing about," she said between sobs.

"Come in, come in," she told them and as they passed, she threw her arms around Imary, and then Edward. "Hello grandma," they both said.

Mrs Chisholm then noticed the Wilkie family standing to the side with Bruin. "Oh, please, come in all of you. And Bruin as well, of course. All of this is thanks to all of you."

The family walked in to the house and found the others in the sitting room.

As Mrs Chisholm entered the room, Mrs Wilkie said: "We don't want to get in the way of your reunion so we'll hand over the treasure box straight away and then let you get to know each other.

"Have you got the box, Harriet?"

"Here it is," said Harriet as she handed the box to Mrs Chisholm.

"These things are all yours and we've looked after them since you saw them at the hospital."

Mrs Chisholm said "thank you so very much. But please don't go."

Mrs Chisholm sat on the sofa, in between Imary and Edward and untied the ribbon and opened the box.

She gasped as she again saw the photograph,

the cufflinks and pearls, the pen and the three shiny silver coins.

Finally she unwrapped the last, smallest package and there it was: her diamond and sapphire engagement ring which her husband had accused Matthew of stealing all those years ago.

"When I saw this in the hospital I didn't believe it and I still find it hard to believe it is real," she said through tears as she unwrapped the ring. "Oh, Matthew. How can you ever forgive me? You always said you hadn't taken the ring but Arthur was so sure you had stolen it."

"There's nothing to forgive, mum. I'm just so glad it's been found and we have come together at last," said Matthew.

"And it's all thanks to you," Mrs Chisholm said, looking at the Wilkie children.

"And to Bruin of course after I had that fall and he found me. It's all too much to take in."

Mrs Wilkie and the children all had to wipe away tears as they listened to Mrs Chisholm.

"I think we'll get away now and let you get to know your family properly," said Mrs Wilkie.

But Henry had spotted a huge chocolate cake, covered in cream and chocolate sprinkles. "What about the cake?" he asked. "Oh Henry, come on. It's time for us to go," said his mother.

"Nonsense," said Matthew. "The least you deserve is a slice of cake. And we would all love to hear all the details about finding the treasure box and about Bruin saving mum."

And so the family sat down to cake and tea and told the story of Bruin and the buried treasure, right from when Mr Wilkie told the family about the children in Spain finding the Roman coins.

"Thank you," said Matthew afterwards. "For helping save mum after her fall and for reuniting the family after all these years.

"We'll make sure we never lose touch again. It's been quite an eventful time for you all and the star of the show has been Bruin. You must be very proud of him."

"We are," said Florence.

"And we never know what is next around the corner for Bruin or any of us. We're just so pleased to have helped."

Bruin went over to Mrs Chisholm and rested his head in her lap where she rubbed his ears and looked into his eyes.

She told him: "Thank you Bruin. You may not have become a police dog but you truly are a wonder dog!"

19

Back At Home

The Wilkie family waved goodbye to the Chisholms as they got back into their car for the short ride home.

Matthew had presented the children with £20 each as a thank you for finding the treasure box and for getting in touch with him and getting the family reunited.

Mrs Wilkie had told him "that's not necessary, we're just delighted to see everything has worked out so well."

Henry stared at his mother with a frown but thankfully Matthew had insisted on handing over the reward..

"We can pay daddy back now for the metal detector. We still owe him £48.50," said Harriet.

"And that will leave £11.50 for us to share," said Florence, who did the maths in her head.

When they returned home they were still feeling very excited about their day and seeing not only Matthew, but his wife and children as well.

It made all of them think of how important keeping in touch with your family was.

Mr Wilkie rang up to ask how it had gone and said he was going to take the afternoon off and come home to share in their high spirits.

As he walked through the front door half an hour later the children ran to greet him and Florence very proudly handed over the £48.50 which they still owed for the metal detector.

"That's really good of you all but it seems a bit mean for me to take it after all you've done. I tell you what, let's all go out for a real treat and spend this money!

"How about a visit to the water park in the next town and have a go on everything?

"It's a lovely day and that would be a great way to spend an afternoon of the school holidays!" he said.

Within minutes towels and swimming costumes were found and the family was ready to go.

Bruin was happy to stay at home in his bed – he knew he wouldn't be allowed into the water park – and as the family set off for their great day out he lazily stretched out for a quiet and peaceful afternoon.

They returned home exhausted but very happy and were greeted by Bruin as he climbed out of his bed to say hello.

As soon as they entered the water park the children ran to the biggest slide – called the Demon Drop – and started to climb the steps to the platform,

The slide started with a jet of water shooting at the back of the rider and forcing up the speed. Then as the rider gathered speed it looked like you were going over the edge of the world.

In fact, the slide continued as soon as you went over the edge and there was the steepest drop you'd ever seen as you went over the other side.

Henry got to the platform but then lost his nerve. "I'm not going down. It's too fast," he said, shaking as he spoke.

Thankfully there was an attendant who pointed to a staircase which Henry was able to walk down and as he looked back he saw Florence and then Harriet both go down the Demon Drop.

Both girls screamed as they went over the edge and then down the almost vertical slide, ending up in a deep pool and swimming to the edge.

"That was brilliant, let's go again!" said Florence and Harriet agreed.

"But I want to go on the teacups ride," said Mrs Wilkie. "Henry will go with you," shouted Florence as she and Harriet ran back to the steps to the Demon Drop.

They both climbed back to the top, from where they could see their parents and Henry climbing into one of the teacups which gently took them on a ride around the park.

"Me first this time," said Harriet as they took off at the start of the ride.

Florence followed and again both girls screamed loud enough to be heard back in Tingleside as they shot over the edge.

The family had great fun at the water park and as well as paying for all their entry fees, Matthew's money let them all have a slap up tea as well.

They returned home exhausted but very happy and were greeted by Bruin as he climbed out of his bed to say hello.

The children gathered around him to tell him what a great afternoon they had had.

"Oh Bruin," said Florence. "We knew we would love you but we never knew what excitement there would be."

Harriet agreed. "I wonder what's next?" she said.

But no-one knew the answer to that and as the light outside began to fade it was time for baths and bed to end a brilliant day.

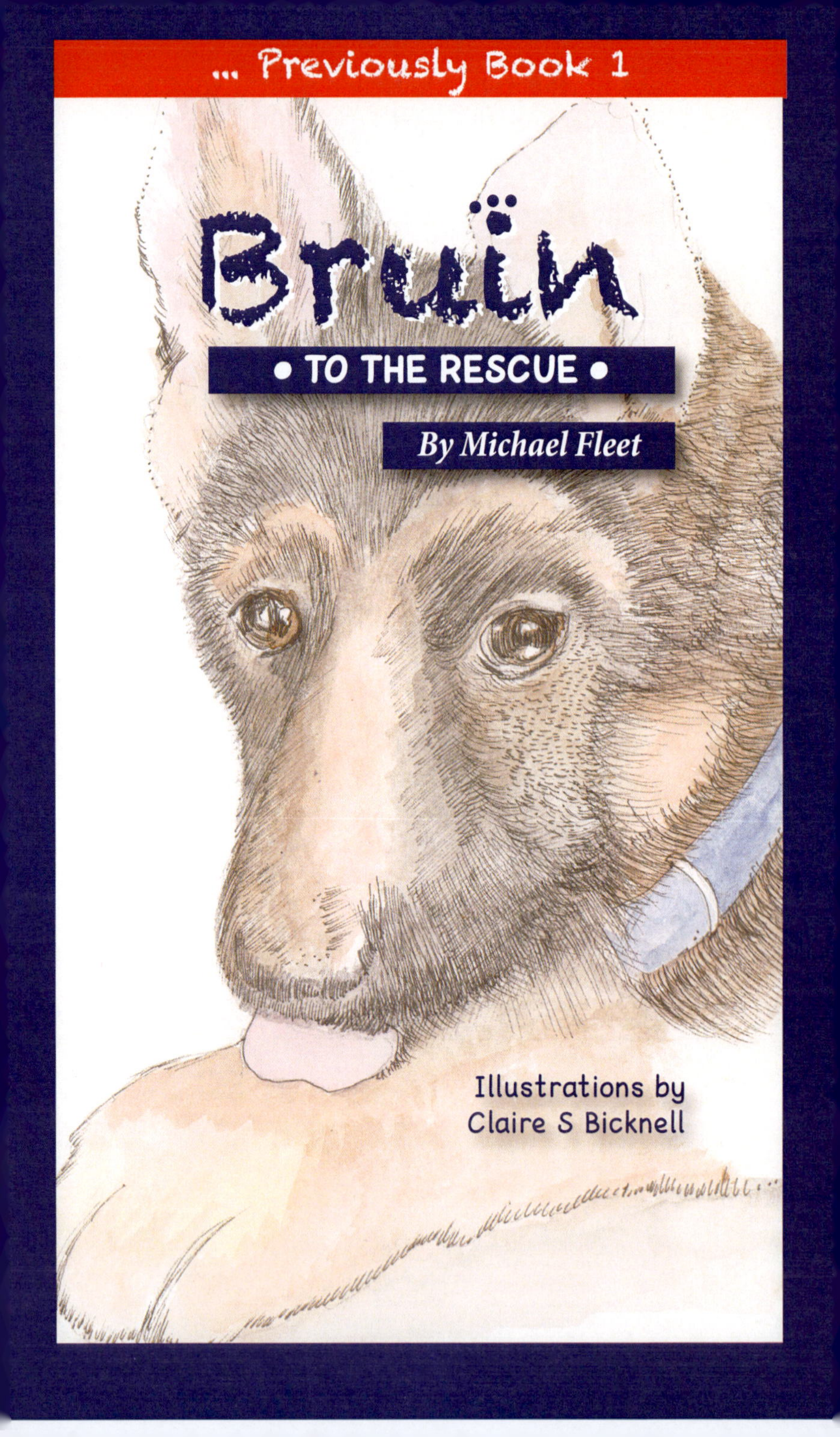
... Previously Book 1
Bruin
TO THE RESCUE
By Michael Fleet
Illustrations by
Claire S Bicknell

... Coming soon Book 3

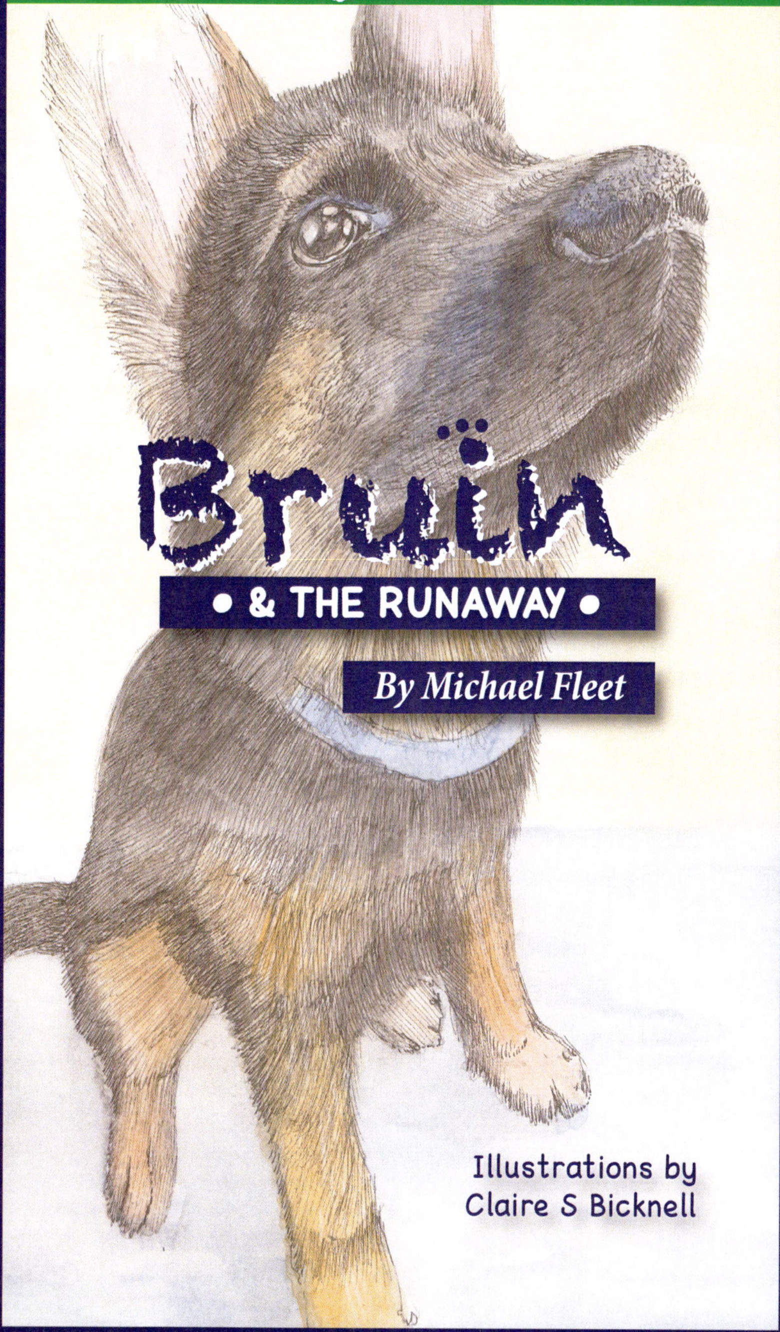

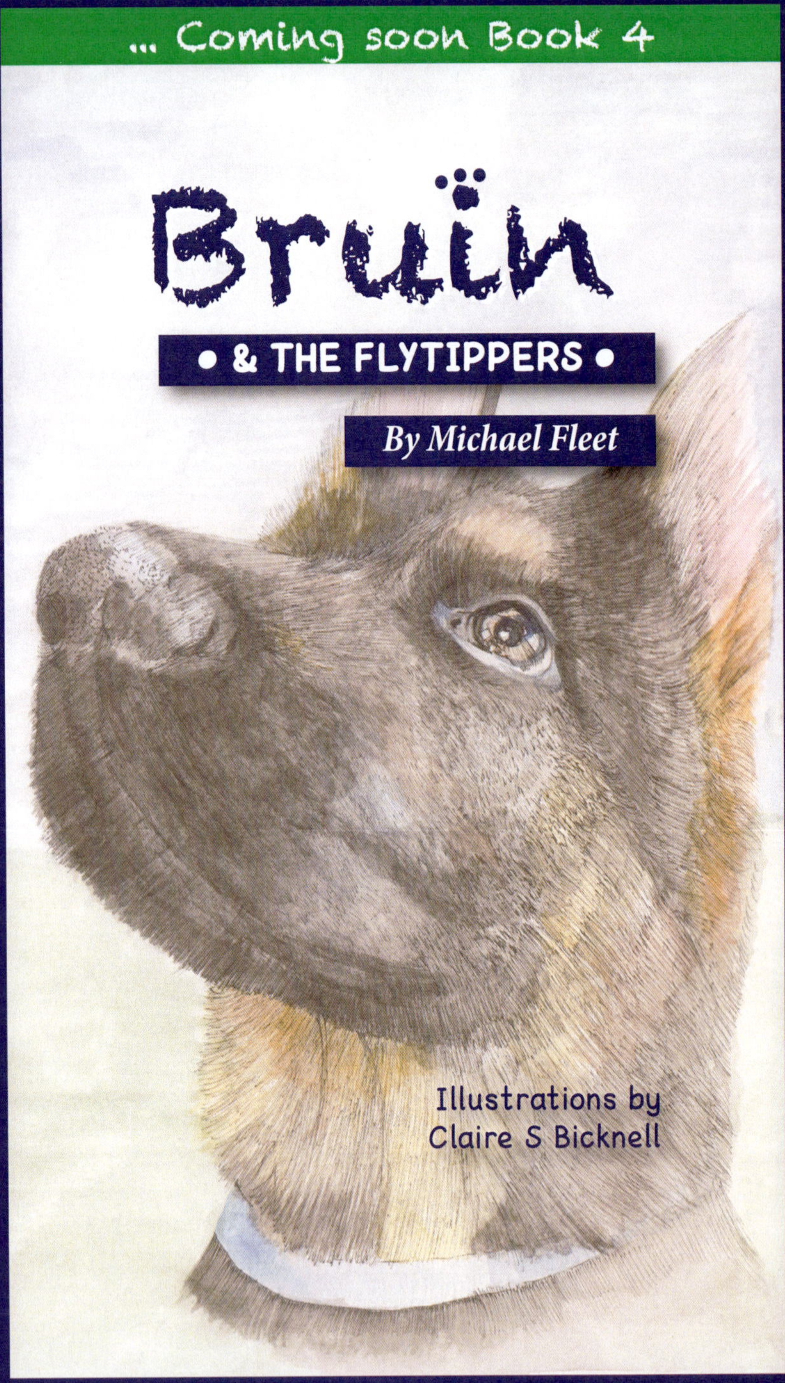
... Coming soon Book 4
Bruïn
• & THE FLYTIPPERS •
By Michael Fleet
Illustrations by
Claire S Bicknell

... Coming soon Book 5

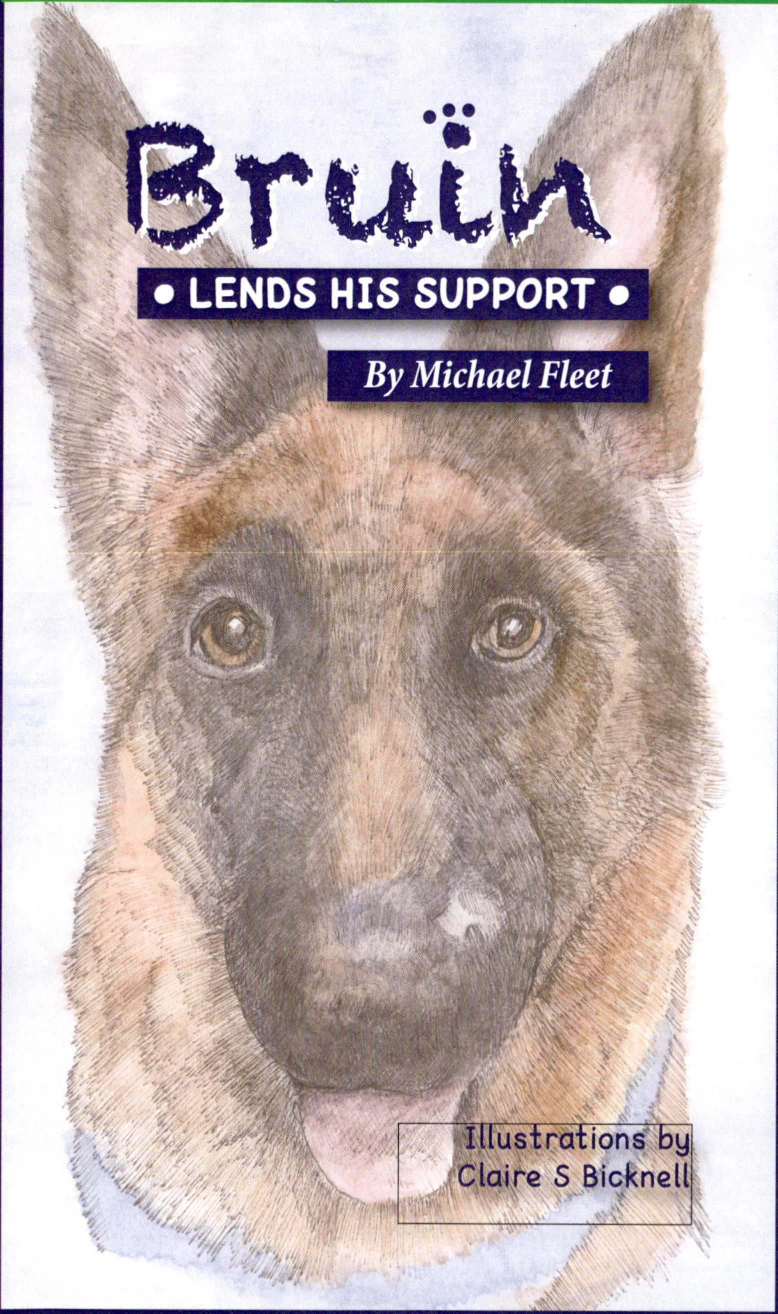

Photography © Charlie Hudson: Nala

About The Author

Michael Fleet is a retired journalist living in Cornwall where he ran a B&B with his wife, Babs.

He has four grandchildren – three girls and one boy – and decided to create the Bruin adventure series after reading about an award winning police dog in Germany which had been retired and given to a family as a pet after becoming too friendly and lovable.

Among other passtimes, he enjoys walking on the beach with his own dog, Maisie.

Photography © Michael Fleet – his own dog Maisie

Metal Detecting as a hobby!

Adults and children alike will love the thrill of finding treasure in the shape of coins, nails or a rusty old key! Its outdoors and healthy fun and equipment can be purchased for modest outlay as a Birthday or Gift that keeps on giving...

Darren – Bournmouths Treasure Hunter

Metal detecting is a fun outdoor activity and, occasionally, a profitable one!

Metal detectors can be bought from specialist shops or websites or from auction sites, like ebay, where they are often cheaper but might not be as good quality.

When starting out with a metal detector, new owners will often search their own garden and, even here, some treasure can be found. One child, who we will call Simon, found a Roman coin in his own back garden, but mostly you will find things like rusty nails and old bits of tin!

Once you are ready to explore further afield the beach is a good place to try as you do not need written permission to search there. (If you are searching in a farmer's field or in public places like parks you will need the permission of the land owner or the local council.)

All sorts of things can be found on the beach and one person, Darren Wiles, has set up a group of volunteers to find things people have lost on one of England's largest beaches, at Bournemouth.

People have asked him to find all sorts of things, from rings or necklaces to mobile phones or watches. "It is the best feeling in the world when you find a treasured item for someone," said Darren.

In his time he has found a Cartier bracelet and a Rolex watch, each worth about £10,000, and on another occasion he found two rings which were precious possessions given to two sisters before their mother passed away. "Sometimes these things are not just valuable but hold precious memories for the person who has lost them," he said.

He uses a metal detector made by a company called Go-Find and recommends their equipment for anyone starting out. They even have a starter set specially for children and can be found in the UK at crawfordsmd.com.

His main piece of advice for a child starting out with a metal detector is simply "get out there and have fun. You will soon learn the sounds made by different objects and who knows what you will find? I love it and hope you will too!" said Darren.

Photography © Claire S Bicknell: Raffi & Sebastian hunting treasure!

How to ADOPT a Retired Police Dog?

It is possible to give a home to one of the dozens of police dogs who retire each year or to those, like Bruin, who begin their training but are not suited to a life in the police force.

Some of these may have a physical problem, such as weak hips or other joints, while others will just not have the determination or character needed by the police. And most of these are similar to Bruin in that they are just too gentle for a career in the police!

For anyone looking to adopt a "too nice" police dog or one which has retired at the end of its career the best thing to do is contact your local police dog handling team and register your interest.

The police screen all applicants to make sure they are up to the job of looking after one of these very special dogs and, if an animal becomes available, people on the waiting list will be contacted.

Some owners of retired police dogs are supported by charities which raise money to help with vets bills as these dogs are often not able to be insured and these groups help raise awareness of the need for homes for the dogs.

In England one such charity is WAGS Retired Police Dogs, which supports police dogs from Wiltshire, Avon, Gloucestershire and Somerset and a proportion of the proceeds of all Bruin books will be given to the charity to help with their work.

Graham Heathfield chairman of the charity, said "most retired police dogs go on to live with their handler but some of those which do not make it as police dogs are adopted by other families, such as the Wilkies who gave Bruin a safe and loving home.

And while there is no guarantee that the dogs will have adventures like Bruin's all will make very special pets!"

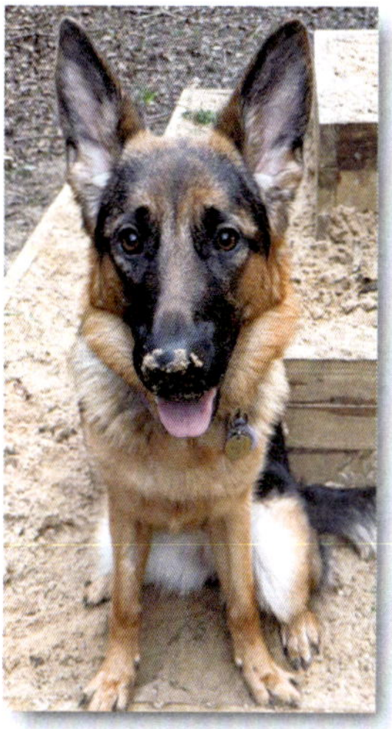

For more information you can check the WAGS website on

wagsretiredpolicedogs.co.uk

or the National Federation for Retired Service Animals, which looks after dogs from the police, fire service, prison service or border force, on:

nfrsa.org.uk.

Alternatively contact your local police dog handling team.

Book Three in the Adventures of Bruin series is Bruin and the Runaway! which is available through Amazon or direct from the author (signed if required) at:

bruinstories@gmail.com

Photography © Charlie Hudson: Nala

How can you support Retired Police Dogs?

PC Robin Dimond has been a police Dog Handler, for the past 16 years. He spent 15 of those as a Dog Handler recently moving into the training team.

His role consists of bringing on new potential police dogs for the first year of their lives until they are old enough to complete an Initial Police Dog Course.

He trains both General Purpose Police dogs and specialist Search Explosive dogs.

Chris Davis has been a police officer for 24 years. A dog handler for the past 14 years.

He handles a German Shepherd called Wilson, who is a 7 year old Firearm Support dog and Rocky (Spaniel) a 7 year old specialist drug/cash/firearm recovery dog.

Both Chris and Rob operate within the Dog Support Unit of Hampshire and Isle of Wight Constabulary.

The Hants charity set up and run by some of the current and retired handlers is: **Pension4Paws.**

They support retired Police dogs with vet bills and rehoming etc.

https://pensions4paws.com/

A Police dog handler and his dog always form a close bond.

Photography © Dave Pimbblet

Photography © Dave Pimbblet

POLICE
3346

Chris Davis has been a police officer for 24 years. A dog handler for the past 14 years.

Photography © Dave Pimbblet

Colouring Pages

Please have fun adding your own ideas to our illustrations...Make Bruin your own!

Illustration © Claire S Bicknell

Illustration © Claire S Bicknell

Illustration © Claire S Bicknell

Illustration © Claire S Bicknell

We would love to see your colouring-in and hear your ideas for future adventures with Bruin.

Please do send screen shots of your colouring of these illustrations or ones of your own inspired by these stories together with any ideas or comments you may have to the Author:

Email Michael Fleet: bruinstories@gmail.com
(under 18 years old, please seek prior written permission from your parents or carers)